EDIBLE
LANDSCAPING

URBAN FOOD GARDENS THAT LOOK GREAT

SENGA LINDSAY

EDIBLE LANDSCAPING

URBAN FOOD GARDENS THAT LOOK GREAT

HARBOUR PUBLISHING CO. LTD.

Harbour Publishing Co. Ltd.
P.O. Box 219, Madeira Park, BC, V0N 2H0
www.harbourpublishing.com

Cover photograph © judywhite / Garden Photos.com
Author photo, back cover © *North Shore News* / Mike Wakefield
Page 2 © iStockphoto.com / Aleksei Potov
Edited by Carol Pope and Cliff Rowlands
Cover and Text design by Five Seventeen
Printed and bound in Canada

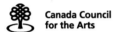 

Harbour Publishing acknowledges financial support from the Government of Canada through the Canada Book Fund and the Canada Council for the Arts, and from the Province of British Columbia through the BC Arts Council and the Book Publishing Tax Credit.

LIBRARY AND ARCHIVES CANADA CATALOGUING IN PUBLICATION

Lindsay, Senga
Edible landscaping : urban food gardens that look great / Senga Lindsay.

Includes index.
ISBN 978-1-55017-580-6

1. Urban gardening.
2. Vegetable gardening.
3. Fruit-culture.
4. Herb gardening.
I. Title.

SB453.L55 2012   635.091732   c2012-900322-0

DEDICATION

For the many people in my life who have directly and indirectly made it possible and cheered me on when I had my doubts—I won't name names for fear of leaving someone out! However, special thoughts go out to my mom (Matilda) and dad (John), who fostered my creative spirit and love of horticulture and nature at a very young age, inspiring me to follow the path I remain on to this day.

ACKNOWLEDGEMENTS

A book like this does not come together without the hard work of a great team. My sincere thanks goes out to all those involved in its creation: To my editors, Carol Pope and Cliff Rowlands, for not only perfectly distilling my words but patiently educating and guiding me through the world of book publishing. To everyone at Harbour Publishing for all their support and faith in bringing this book to reality. To Teresa Karbashewski for providing the beautiful illustrations and capturing the essence of my designs. To Berglind Hendrickson for "cracking the whip" and getting all the venues lined up so that people know the book is "out there"! And, of course, to Five Seventeen for his exciting design work.

CONTENTS

©iStockPhoto.com/FenWiedemann

PREFACE

Gone are the days when an urban gardener had to choose between growing edibles or having a well-groomed outdoor space. With over 25 years of experience in landscape architecture, arboriculture and horticultural planning, author Senga Lindsay has created 15 inspiring designs to simplify the answer to the question of how to make food gardens fabulous. *Edible Landscaping: Urban Food Gardens That Look Great* clearly shows us how to lay out vegetable, fruit and herb gardens so that they look wonderful all year round.

Whether you want to grow an edible rooftop or living wall, European potager, permaculture or herb patch, raised square-foot bed, allotment crops or collection of containers on a balcony, Senga—winner of multiple awards for her sustainable-design work—offers insight on how to plan and plant a garden that will hold its own through the seasons. Starting with her secrets to organizing any outdoor space, this invaluable guide moves into the essentials of each design, with tips on maximizing beauty and bounty.

Form and function are paramount throughout, with strategies included for facilitating gardeners with mobility, vision or memory challenges. Cost efficient and adaptable, each plan can adjust to a smaller space or large—the urban courtyard, for example, is stunning as a stand-alone retreat or outdoor "room" within the larger landscape. Fencing, outbuildings, seating, pathways and finishing touches are noted, along with soil, irrigation and maintenance recommendations. Children are honoured with a mix of hideaways, mazes, pizza patches, and mini and monster plantings. And a backyard gourmet kitchen walled with easy-grow vertical plantings takes every aspect of the garden-to-table experience outdoors.

As a garden editor, it's clear to me that more and more city dwellers are seeking to lower grocery bills, reduce their carbon footprint and enjoy the health incentives and unbeatable flavour of organic produce fresh from the garden—all the while, discovering how incredibly gratifying it is to grow their own. *Edible Landscaping: Urban Food Gardens That Look Great* empowers us all to be able to enjoy a stunning outdoor space while reaping the many benefits that come hand in hand with harvesting our own homegrown food.

—Carol Pope

The author's garden—you can have a stylish garden and eat out of it, too!

INTRODUCTION

As a landscape architect I have seen many trends come and go in garden design. But none have been as popular as the edible garden. In almost every project, be it a private residence or a condominium complex, a vegetable or community garden is always at the top of the wish list. But this "wish" is always qualified with such comments as "I want it to look beautiful and not like a typical (translation: messy) vegetable garden," or "I want to grow a few vegetables but not have my whole space taken up by it," and, finally, "I have a limited amount of time but want to grow some tomatoes and a few other favourite veggies."

Chances are you reside in the city or suburbs. And for most of us that means we are living an urban lifestyle that is hectic, stressful and in a state of continual information overload. You don't have a lot of time to research every nuance of designing an outdoor space, yet want to experience the simpler pleasures of growing and harvesting food and fixing garden-fresh meals for family and friends. And you want your garden to be a retreat, a place to recharge and relax.

This book is a culmination of my 25-plus years of experience as a landscape architect and horticulturist specializing in all things edible—from designing chic outdoor spaces that do double duty as a food garden to growing easy and delicious edibles that are a stylish addition to your garden and table.

In short, think of this book as a fast track to creating a beautiful outdoor space brimming with edibles that you can enjoy with family and friends within your first season! Enjoy.

—Senga Lindsay

Using simple design strategies, edible gardens can be both beautiful and functional.

©Senga Lindsay

YOU! AS A DESIGNER

Have you ever sat in your outdoor space musing "What if I made my deck larger so I have a place to put a proper table for eating outside?" "What if I add a vegetable patch so I can serve my guests food fresh from the garden?" Whether you realize it or not, you have been visually rearranging your outdoor space and coming up with ideas for improvements. This is no different from what a professional designer does. A designer simply works through these same questions, using a four-step approach.

Designing your edible garden or outdoor space is comparable to planning a new kitchen. By working through a process, you can save valuable time, materials and resources. Planning ahead avoids costly mistakes—especially if you are putting in semi-permanent features such as walls, landscape structures or flooring that would be difficult and expensive to relocate.

This process also helps you to crystallize, in your own mind, what you want in terms of a space both specific to your needs and reflecting your style. That ultra-minimalist landscape might look great in a magazine but how will it work with your family's needs? And how durable might it be or comfortable to live in?

It's also important to do a reality check to determine how much time you are willing to commit to maintaining your landscape. Gardens, and particularly edible ones, are dynamic and ever-changing and usually require attention a few hours a week.

At the end of this process you will have a master plan complete with drawings you can build from over time. Most of us do not have the time or funds to undertake a large project all at once. This document becomes a comprehensive guide that will help you stay with your vision as you breathe new life into your outdoor space.

The smallest space can become a perfect oasis for relaxing and entertaining.

Planted right, edibles become living art.

THE FOUR STEPS

The secret to good garden design—similar to those landscapes we pore over in garden magazines—is a carefully thought-out plan. This involves assessing and analyzing the site, deciding what to include, and matching ideas with the suitability of the space. Once you arrive at an appropriate garden concept, "the rubber hits the road."

1. DO YOUR HOMEWORK

Don't be blinded by what you currently see in your yard. View it as a clean slate—forget the dilapidated deck, broken-down shed or whatever it is you are harbouring in your backyard. When I look at a client's yard, I see the possibilities first and so should you—now is not the time to limit yourself.

This is where the homework starts. Make a scrapbook diary to record all your thoughts and ideas. Copy or cut out and paste images that inspire you, from books, magazines or the Internet (search "images" on Google and check out Flickr).

Use your scrapbook to answer the following important questions:

WHAT IS YOUR LIFESTYLE?

Take an inventory of your life. Do you live alone or with a partner? Children? Pets? Do you enjoy parties or prefer quiet dinners with friends and family? Once you understand what makes you (and your family) tick, and what you need to enjoy your garden space, then the design process can begin.

WHAT IS YOUR WISH LIST?

Record all the elements you would like to see in your landscape. For example, have you always wanted an outdoor kitchen or large dining space complete with fireplace? It can be as specific or broad-based as you like. A space to gather? A wildlife haven? Strictly an area to grow food?

WHAT MAKES YOU HAPPY?

Picture your idea of heaven, be it a jungle of lush foliage set around a tranquil pool and replete with waterfall spilling into a hot tub, or an outdoor dining room below a jasmine-covered arbour lit by an overhead chandelier.

Do not limit yourself to the garden—visualize places or scenes that make you joyous or at peace. I adore France, so the ultimate for me is to share a bottle of wine and fresh-sliced tomatoes drizzled with olive oil and balsamic vinegar with friends on a veranda under a shady arbour, reminiscent of when I did the same in Provence. These are the types of experiences you may wish to emulate in your own outdoor spaces. Pay attention to sights, sounds, sensations, smells and even tastes—these all play a role in how your garden will sing to your senses.

WHAT IS YOUR STYLE?

Your sense of style is very much influenced by such things as history and fashion and is reflected in your choices in everything from architecture to clothing to furniture to cars and even appliances!

Garden style refers to the way we express ideas in terms of organizing the outdoor space we use for recreation, meditation, entertaining or as a backdrop to a building. The materials, plant palette, colours and ornamentation and how they are laid out in the landscape help to create this style. Throughout history, distinct garden styles have been created and are easily recognizable because their creators commonly drew inspiration from familiar culture, architectural and historical references. For example, formal gardens reminiscent of old English, French and Italian estates are rooted in classical architecture and design dating back to antiquity. Order, repetition and axial symmetry are all devices used to create strict visual and spatial balance.

In contrast, while the modernist garden style is frequently limited in its variety of plants and hard surfaces in a manner similar to the formal garden, its spaces are generally free-flowing and asymmetrical. And the material palette is minimal, with polished concrete often used for paving, walls and other hard surfaces, with little or no decoration.

We look to historical gardens as inspirations for our own landscape spaces, into which we inject our personalities and modern-day requirements. In designer talk, we call this the "theme" or "concept" of

A strong theme, as shown in this modern-style outdoor room, is the key to successful design.

the garden. A strong theme is the difference between a mediocre and stunning result.

As part of your scrapbook, gather visuals of specific gardens or related ideas. Try to find images of your ultimate dream garden. No detail is insignificant—in addition to the big picture, gather ideas for pots, patio furniture and plant combinations.

> Tip: Take time to visit garden centres and bring along your digital camera and notepad—this is an ideal way to get ideas first-hand, from pots to plant combinations to ornaments or furniture.

WHAT IS YOUR TIME COMMITMENT?

Confused and overwhelmed by the plethora of images, styles or ideas that you have recorded in your scrapbook? Don't panic! There are more steps to go through in this design process before you start to pin down your final vision. And one very important consideration, which is what is realistic based on your schedule.

There's no way around it—the bigger your garden the more time you need to devote to looking after it. Don't kid yourself: if you can only spare a couple hours a week, think about a courtyard approach or container plantings instead of a large traditional row or potager garden.

Fact: A conventional single-row garden needs approximately 2 hours of maintenance per week spring through fall for each 100 sq. ft. (9 sq. m).

WHAT IS YOUR BUDGET?

Another reality check is budget. Formulate a rough idea of how much you want to spend. Typically 60 percent is set aside for soft works with the remainder for hard landscaping. Soft works include soil excavation and plantings; hard landscaping encompasses decking, paving and walls.

In terms of making a good investment decision, a rule of thumb is to plan to spend no more than 15 to 20 percent of the capital value of your property on landscaping. The costs of landscape design can also be staggered over months or years. A budget can help you to prioritize the work to be completed, organizing it into phases that take place over a short or long time frame.

2. TAKE INVENTORY OF YOUR SITE

This stage requires you to use your powers of observation to record sun patterns, temperature fluctuations and the existing plants in the area you are considering—all clues to what is likely to survive there. Are there microclimates? Easements? Access issues? There is a lot to consider.

Record your observations on a scale drawing of your site. Use grid or graph paper with quarter-inch squares, with each square representing one foot. If you are computer savvy there are a number of landscape-design software packages available. Show all the correct sizes and locations of the existing elements on your site. This will provide you with a base for your final master plan.

CLIMATE AND GROWING CONDITIONS
WEATHER

Where are the prevailing winds? When and how much does it rain? How often do you get frost?

SOIL DRAINAGE

Do have clay or sandy soil? Are there wet spots in the garden? Will you need to build raised beds?

VEGETATION

Are there existing trees or shrubs you want to retain?

ORIENTATION AND SEASONAL ISSUES

Does the house shade parts of the garden? Do deciduous plants let in light during winter? Does one side of the house or garden get hot in summer? These are especially important issues for planning a vegetable garden.

MICROCLIMATES

South-facing walls that gather heat can be used to grow tender crops. Low-lying sheltered corners may be sun traps in summer but frost pockets in winter.

SHADOWS

Your house and outbuildings can cast shadows that affect your garden's light in varying ways depending on the time of the year.

BUILDINGS AND EASEMENTS

EASEMENTS, CAVEATS AND UTILITIES

Are there legal restrictions on what you can do and where you can build? Look for gas, electricity, phone, sanitary and water connections that you will need to be careful to avoid.

EXISTING BUILDINGS AND HARD SURFACES

Are there sheds, paved areas, or garden beds to work into your plan?

FUTURE ADDITIONS

Will there be any future additions or renovations (extra rooms, new garage, etc.)?

OTHER CONSIDERATIONS

- Is there a slope or change in levels?
- Can vehicles or pedestrians have good access?
- Are there pavers, timber or any other reusable resources on the site?

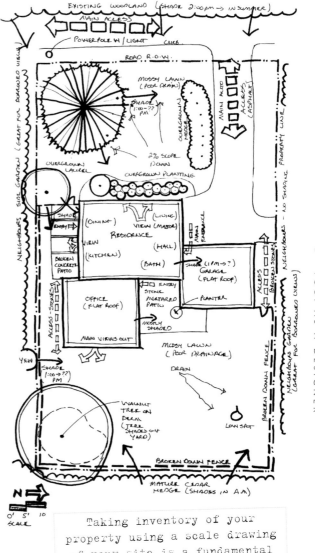

Taking inventory of your property using a scale drawing of your site is a fundamental step in the design process.

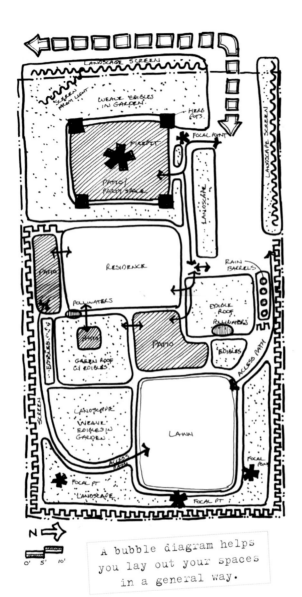

A bubble diagram helps you lay out your spaces in a general way.

3. LAY IT ALL ON PAPER

Now, using tracing paper that can overlay your site plan, start to clarify your thoughts with bubble diagrams that identify areas for different activities such as eating, dining, seating, play spaces or that vegetable garden you are wishing for. In short, think about your garden as a series of outdoor rooms. Just like your house, each room should have a particular purpose: like the lounge room indoors, the patio outside may be the place to relax with guests. Like the dining room indoors, the courtyard may be where you have a sit-down dinner.

Be sure to include routes or connections between the bubbles, as these will be important in helping you connect spaces and determine a practical circulation pattern. Other notes to include are areas that need screening, focal points, or view corridors that should be left open.

Experiment to your heart's content—this is an ideal way to explore different options. Ultimately, you will choose the configuration that feels right.

4. ARRIVE AT THE MASTER PLAN

From the bubble diagram, we progress to a working plan—a two-dimensional representation of a three-dimensional garden. This plan should be drawn precisely to scale, as you or a contractor will be building from it. By bringing all your ideas together on paper you can determine if they are viable within your particular space.

Order and repetition of vertical and horizontal elements can contribute to a compelling edible garden design.

WHAT TO INCLUDE

SINGLE ELEMENTS

Include your pond, stepping stones, lights, drainage inlets, plants (individual trees and plants), firepits, fireplaces, pots, etc.

VERTICAL ELEMENTS

Consider fences, walls, vertical plantings, steps, etc.

Tip: Use landscape features (walls, arbours, etc.) or softer material such as plants and trees to provide vertical and horizontal enclosures. As in your house, this will help define your "rooms."

HORIZONTAL ELEMENTS

Include patios, arbours, kitchens, planting beds, etc.

Tip: You may also want to create a separate planting plan for beds, as this section of your plan can become quite cluttered if there are a lot of plants. A planting plan is important for calculating the correct number of plants for each garden and identifying their exact locations. Use the ultimate mature size of the plants to avoid planting a garden that will be overgrown in a few years. You can also enlarge your scale to "blow up" key areas in your garden that require greater detailing—such as the layout of an edible garden.

Consistency in layout and materials can make a
traditional edible garden a feast for the eyes.

ANATOMY OF AN EDIBLE GARDEN

THE BONES

Although one of your main goals may be to grow a diversity of food for your table, the reason you are reading this book is that you don't want your yard to look like a "dog's breakfast"—messy, unkempt and utilitarian. The most important design elements for an edible landscape are distinctive lines and structure. Because edible plantings usually encompass a more varied mix of textures, forms and colours than a typical ornamental landscape, it in fact helps to almost over-emphasize the "bone structure" of your landscape; otherwise it can become just another scraggly vegetable patch.

Use pathways, patios, planters, hedges, evergreens and any number of structures to provide a sense of continuity and beauty through the seasonal flowering, fruiting and ever-changing colour and foliage, including those less-dramatic in-between times of harvesting, transplanting and pre-season preparation.

CHOOSING YOUR CROP

One common mistake gardeners make is over-planting the vegetables they like to eat, or underestimating what an edible can produce. Unless you absolutely love the very prolific zucchini, one plant may be enough even for a family of four. List the vegetables your family most likes to eat and then start with a small number to test the results.

Don't forget that edibles can double as ornamentals. For example, grapes can replace traditional vining plants for arbours and screening. Kale, Swiss chard and lettuce are available in an array of colours and can be striking bedding plants. And I always include edible flowers in my garden—they are great multi-taskers, providing food and cut flowers, attracting pollinating and beneficial insects, and working as companion plants that repel many plant pests and diseases.

Kale is the ultimate "bomb-proof" edible. And from a designer point of view, the plethora of leaf colours, shapes and sizes makes it highly ornamental in the garden. In pots it is the perfect filler plant: combine it with other beautiful cool-season greens such as Swiss chard, and the textures and colours will play off of each other. Dwarf varieties can be grown in containers as small as 6 in. (15 cm).

Best grown in full sun, marigolds repel insects from other edibles and their petals add a citrus flavour to salads.

THE RIGHT SPACING

With edibles, always make your plans based on the mature size of the plant. While it may be hard to imagine that a tiny cucumber seedling will ultimately grow 3–4 ft. (90–120 cm) in all directions, trust me, it will!

WHAT SIZE?

It's okay to start small. A plot just 10 × 12 ft. (3 × 3.5 m) is sufficient for a garden sampler with a variety of greens, herbs, a few tomatoes, peppers, beans, cucumbers, basil, parsley and edible flowers. A garden 20 × 20 ft. (6 × 6 m) will give you room for a wide range of crops, including some that require a lot of space, such as sweet corn and winter squash.

THE ESSENTIALS

SUN

Most edibles require a minimum of six hours of sunlight a day. Plan to place the majority of your garden for maximum sunlight. And for less than ideal conditions look to shade-tolerant edibles such as kale, lettuce and Oriental greens.

WATER

Consider how you wish to irrigate your crops. Strategically placed taps or hoses are much easier than lugging buckets of water. If your garden is large or you are pressed for time, seriously consider an automatic irrigation system.

ACCESS

Ponder the distance between the kitchen and garden— the closer they are to each other, the more likely you

©fotolia.com/Martin Kemp

Woven cloches are ornamental and protect tender seedlings.

are to dash out for herbs for supper on a rainy day. Pathways and bed widths need to be designed for wheelbarrow access and easy reach. Use the 3-foot rule for both—3 ft. (90 cm) for paths and 3 ft. (90 cm) for the width of beds (4 ft./120 cm when there is access from both sides).

STORAGE AND OUTBUILDINGS

Even if you have only a few pots, you need to consider where to store basic tools and supplies. If your garden is extensive, a garden shed, a place for composting and a greenhouse may be considered must-haves and should be conveniently placed into your plan.

Permanent paving and bed treatments can unify
and enhance an edible garden while making it
a delight to use.

THE TRADITIONAL ROW VEGETABLE GARDEN

This is the no-frills traditional row method of raising fruits and vegetables. Although its origins can be traced back centuries it wasn't until World War I and II that a distinct style and form emerged. Called War Gardens or Food Gardens for Defense, vegetable, fruit and herb gardens were planted by the public in front and back yards, parks, abandoned lots, on city roofs and in any other space available. The objective was to reduce the pressure on the food supply brought on by the war effort. These gardens were also morale boosters, giving the gardeners a sense of empowerment as they planted and harvested—not unlike today.

The layout of these gardens is pleasingly ordered and utilitarian with beds laid out in simple squares or rectangles with pathways between for access. Often an area devoted to composting, a small potting shed, greenhouse or cold frame is integrated into the plan. These gardens are ideal for those with lots of land and time; for a more intensive garden with less space, look to the square foot method (see page 119).

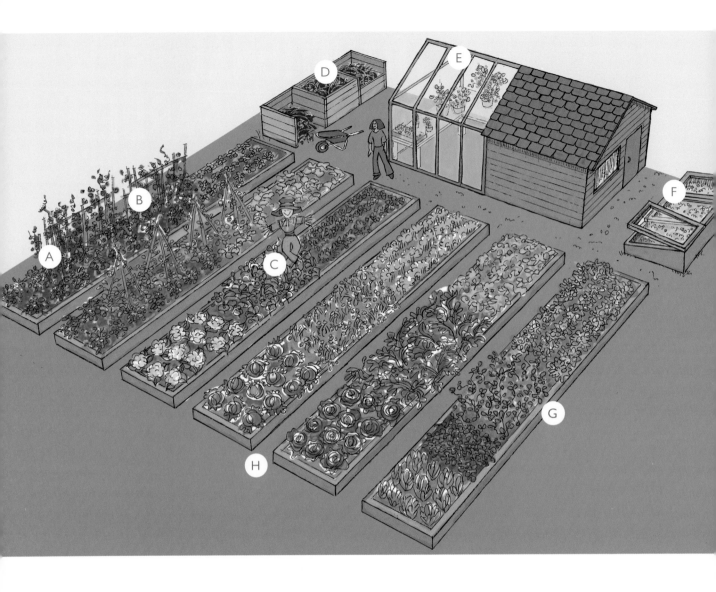

A   Trellises and other vertical elements support vining crops and add dimension to garden space

B   Taller crops are located on the north side of the garden to avoid shading other plants

C   Playful elements provide ornamentation as well as focus and functionality

D   An area for composting is integrated

E   Outbuildings such as greenhouses and potting sheds are invaluable, particularly for the year-round garden

F   Cold frames extend the growing season in the fall and allow seedlings to be started earlier in spring

G   Raised planters (preferably 4 ft./ 120 cm wide and 18 in./45 cm high) filled with good garden soil ensure successful crops

H   Hard-surface pathways a minimum of 3 ft. (90 cm) wide allow for comfortable walking and wheelbarrow access

THE PLAN

Yard Dimensions: 50 × 45 ft. (15 × 14 m)

Total Area of Edibles: 720 sq. ft. (67 sq. m) including cold frame and greenhouse

DESIGN ELEMENTS

THE GARDEN BEDS

A width of 4 ft. (1.2 m) with paths on either side is a good rule of thumb when laying out beds. Any wider and you may need to step into the bed to tend your crops—and all that foot traffic will compact the soil over time and render it useless for growing plants. This measurement is doubly convenient because it can accommodate 3 broccoli plants, cabbages, tomatoes, beans or peas across the bed. Or 5 rows of smaller and more upright growers such as beets, carrots, lettuces or Swiss chard can be squeezed in. Beds may be any length but 30 ft. (9 m) is good to strive for, as it can be divided into 10-ft. (3-m) sections for successive or companion plantings (see page 61).

> Did you know? To provide year-round vegetables for a family of 4 you need about 6 beds, each 30 × 5 ft. (9 × 1.5 m) for a total of 1,100 sq. ft. (100 sq. m).

WALK THIS WAY

Paths need to be 3 ft. (90 cm) wide to accommodate wheelbarrows; their surfaces can be as simple as wood chips, loose stone or even trodden-down soil. Mulches such as straw or bark can also be used and are best laid thickly on top of a weed-suppressing landscape fabric. Note: there are landscape fabrics made from recycled plastic bottles for a more earth-friendly approach.

For a dressier look, use brick or natural stone paths. These materials can also serve as a unifying element in the garden, providing your eye with a

A width of 4 ft. (1.2 m) with paths on either side is a good rule of thumb when laying out garden beds.

bridge that connects one area with another. Unlike soil or mulches, these are permanent paving materials—ensure your bed and path layout are final and use construction techniques (see page 137) appropriate to the materials you select.

GROWING VERTICALLY

One of the best ways to make efficient use of space, especially in a vegetable garden, is to grow edibles vertically. Sprawling vines such as cucumbers and indeterminate tomatoes benefit from being lifted off the ground and away from soil-borne organisms and diseases that can damage your harvest. From a design point of view, all gardens benefit from something that introduces height, interest and rhythm. The contrast of vertical plantings complements the horizontal rows of vegetables and low geometric beds.

The simplest supports are bamboo or wood stakes. However, heavy plants can pull a weak stake out of the ground. If you want a more solid structure, consider using a tripod system. These can be simple rustic wooden stakes or sticks bound at the top with twine.

Tomato cages are also an inexpensive but easy way to support edibles such as tomatoes, eggplants and peppers. Visually they tend to disappear under the growing plants.

© iStockphoto.com/obears99

Prefabricated lattice fencing can be purchased at most building-supply stores.

If aesthetics are not so much a concern, build your own A-frame system, which is very efficient for such vine crops as peas and pole beans. Affix a portion of lattice to a fence or wall, and allow climbing edibles to scramble up. Always remember to match the support to the size of the edible. Thin green netting will not support a hefty tomato plant but will easily do the trick for peas.

ADDITIONAL CONSIDERATIONS

RAISED BEDS

In general, raised beds are the best way to grow the most vegetables with the least amount of work. That's my kind of gardening. The only times I'd recommend not using raised beds is if you have sandy soil, live in a very dry area, or are growing crops that need hilling and mounding, such as potatoes. Otherwise, raise the soil! There are many benefits to raised beds:

- They warm up and dry out faster in spring, so plants get a jump on the season.
- You can grow more vegetables in a smaller space and have less area devoted to paths.

- If your ground is not optimum for growing food, you can simply pour fresh nutrient-filled garden soil right over top of it into your raised beds.
- They create attractive, well-organized planting areas.
- They save on the amount of fertilizer and compost used because it is concentrated on just the planting beds.
- It's less work, especially if you make permanent raised beds bordered with wood, bricks or stone. You won't have to remake the beds each spring.
- The plants will have healthy root systems because you won't be stepping on the planting bed and compacting the soil, which makes it hard for roots to grow.
- You can be more creative with design, making round raised beds, for example, and planting vegetables, herbs and flowers in various designs.
- It's easy to let climbers such as cucumbers grow up an A-frame trellis because it fits nicely over a 3-ft. (90-cm) bed.
- And it is also easy to fit season extenders such as row covers with wire hoops over the 3-ft. (90-cm) beds.
- Most importantly, raised beds are beautiful!

COMPOST BIN AND OUTBUILDINGS

If you have a sizable area and are a real vegetable-garden aficionado you will likely want to include a small compost bin or heap, as well as a shed for potting and the storage of tools, soil and other garden supplies.

GREENHOUSES, COLD FRAMES AND OTHER SEASON EXTENDERS

For those who dream of growing vegetables year round, cold frames and a greenhouse are must-haves. There are myriad choices these days in greenhouses,

Eggplant is a striking filler that comes in a variety of sizes and colours from small and pea-like, to egg-shaped, to long and slender. The fruits offer a stunning colour palette from the traditional royal purple to shades of rose, violet, green, yellow and white, often enhanced with stripes in a contrasting colour. The plants grow from 18 in. (45 cm) to 4 ft. (1.2 m) with large, rangy leaves; flowers are violet-coloured, star-shaped and solitary or in clusters.

from the do-it-yourself kind to portable versions that you can literally inflate and place where you want!

Cold frames are simply miniature greenhouses that protect plants from elements including the weather and critters that munch on plants. With the protection of a cold frame, you can grow plants earlier or later than is possible in an exposed garden space; also, with cold-hardy vegetables you can harvest throughout the winter. In early spring, when the weather can be cold or frosty, cold frames trap heat and keep the soil warm; and throughout the year they maintain moisture that allows seeds to germinate.

For a smaller alternative, a cloche (pronounced closh) can be used to protect individual plants. Traditionally, cloches came in a classical bell-jar shape born of the Victorian era; another variation made from bamboo is woven into an open dome. Both protect

Cloches are highly useful and add ornamentation to your garden.

plants and seedlings from frost and wind-chill yet allow rain to flow through. Fleece or newspaper can be used to cover the plant inside the cloche during periods of heavy frost, but the cloche itself is enough to protect plants on its own from light frosts in spring or fall.

Cloches make great adornments to your garden theme, however this may come at a price, as the beautiful glass cloches are expensive. For those more concerned with function over fashion, though, cloches are relatively easy and inexpensive to create. Simply cut off the bottoms of clear plastic pop bottles and place over your seedlings as desired. Keep in mind that cloches and similar devices will heat up and cool down very quickly, within less than a minute, so regulation of the inside temperature will be tricky during warmer weather. You'll want to make certain the covers are vented to keep plants from wilting under the higher temperatures that can be generated.

Rhubarb forcers—bell-shaped pots with a lid-covered opening at the top—are placed over two- to three-year-old crowns during winter or very early spring to limit the photosynthesis of the plants and encourage tender and sweet blanched stems. Once shoots appear, the lid is removed, causing them to grow toward the light.

A garden teaches a child to respect even the
smallest life, such as an insect or a tiny seedling.

A GARDEN FOR CHILDREN

It is not by accident that I became who I am today—a landscape architect and horticulturist passionate about gardens, nature and growing food. Growing up, my siblings and I were outside from dawn to dusk, playing in the woods behind our parents' house or fishing for pollywogs in the nearby ditches. When I was 11, my dad built me a greenhouse. At one point I had more than 100 potted plants in the house, and the greenhouse was full of seedlings, annuals and perennials that would fill up our yard front and back with a riot of colour.

Research by Dr. Louise Chawla, international coordinator of the Growing Up in Cities program, UNESCO, has shown that children are genetically programmed between ages 6 to 12 to form a bond with nature. This is the natural period where originally our species would have needed to develop survival skills in nature.

With the advent of computers, Internet and video games, children are spending less and less time outside. The result is that they are interacting less and less with our natural environment and in many cases there is a significant disconnect. Without this intrinsic connection, the future of our planet may be in peril—if our children do not understand and become enamoured with the natural environment, who will there be to ensure it is protected for future generations?

A Perimeter fencing doubles as a framework for climbing edibles or espaliered trees

B Outbuildings work as a potting shed and/or children's playhouse

C Adding a green roof to an outbuilding makes it extra environmentally friendly

D Water collection for irrigation (rain barrels)

E Overhead structures create "tunnels" and support edible vines

F Where possible, animal husbandry such as raising chickens is incorporated

G Dwarf fruit trees allow for easy reaching

H Lawn areas allow for children's play

I A pizza garden provides a useful and fun themed centrepiece

J If accessible on all sides, beds are no more than 4 ft. (120 cm) wide to avoid the trampling of crops and soil

K Hard-surface pathways a minimum of 2 ft. (60 cm) wide allow for comfortable walking and wheelbarrow access

L Bean teepees and other hideaways add magic to a children's garden

THE PLAN

Yard Dimensions: 50 × 45 ft. (15 × 14 m)

Total Area of Edibles: 1,500 sq. ft. (140 sq. m)
interspersed throughout garden: Pizza Bed,
4 Raised Beds, Bean Teepee, Fruit Trees and
Planting Beds below

DESIGN ELEMENTS

SECRET HIDEAWAYS

Secret hideaways, garden playrooms and special
structures are enticements that encourage kids to
spend time in the garden—and can transform the
garden into a fantasyland and refuge.

BEAN TEEPEES

Bean teepees are a great way to combine imagination
with food. Pole beans growing on a simple frame will
quickly create a shady hideaway for kids.

What You Need:

- 4 × 4-ft. (1.2 × 1.2-m) garden patch
  suitable for planting
- 8–12 bamboo stakes (at least 6 ft./1.8 m long), or
  for a sturdier structure use 2 × 4 lumber
- String or twine
- Scissors
- Pole bean seeds ('Scarlet Runner' or 'Blue Lake')

Step by Step:

1. When the weather warms up, prepare your area as
   you would any edible garden.
2. Tie stakes together at the top, teepee-style, and set
   them upright in the middle of your garden patch.
   Spread and lightly push the bottom ends of the
   stakes into the ground to make a circle.

Experiment with a combination of plants when creating a bean teepee—gourds, cucumbers, miniature pumpkins or even climbing nasturtiums for lots of colour.

3. Tie twine or string between stakes 4–6 in. (10–
   15 cm) apart to create a mesh for climbing plants.
4. Leave an opening between 2 stakes wide enough
   for a "door" into the teepee.
5. Soak your bean seeds overnight to promote
   germination. Plant 4 or 5 seeds 1 in. (2.5 cm) deep
   at the bottom of each pole.
6. Keep the seeds well watered until they germinate
   and start to climb upward.
7. Thin the seedlings to 2–3 per mound when they
   grow to 3 in. (8 cm) tall. Pinch or cut seedlings at
   ground level when thinning.
8. By midsummer, your bean teepee should be thickly
   covered with foliage (and beans). Use straw or an
   old blanket for the floor.

Adaptable to a wide variety of ornamental uses in the garden, cucumbers are a favourite on my designer list of edibles. Their large lush leaves provide volume and texture to any border and quickly fill and spill over containers or climb up trellises to provide a fast screen in the summertime. While the flowers are small and a subtle yellow, the fruits can be quite striking.

GARDEN TUNNELS

In a sunny area of your garden, make a shady play tunnel for kids to hide in and pumpkins or other vines to grow over!

What You Need:

- 5 × 6 ft. (1.5 x 1.8 m) garden space
- Heavy concrete reinforcement mesh
- Pumpkin, gourd or cucumber seeds
- Rag strips
- Grass clippings or straw

Step by Step:

1. In a sunny area of your garden, have an adult cut a piece of mesh 5 ft. (1.5 m) wide and about 6 ft. (1.8 m) long.
2. Shape the mesh into an arch, pushing the ends of the wire on the 5-ft. (1.5-m) sides into the soil.
3. Plant pumpkin, gourd or cucumber seeds along the sides of the mesh tunnel.
4. As the plants grow, they will cover the mesh and make a fun tunnel to play in! You can tie the plants to the mesh using rag strips if necessary.
5. Cover the floor of your tunnel with grass clippings or straw for comfort.

SUNFLOWER HOUSE OR FORT

These colourful simple "living structures" can be as small as a 4 × 6 ft. (1.2 × 1.8 m) square. Larger 8 × 8 ft. (2.4 × 2.4 m) squares look more convincing as the sunflowers you will use mature at a height of 6–12 ft. (1.8–3.6 m). Sunflowers require relatively little care as long as they have a minimum 6 hours of direct sunlight.

What You Need:

- Sunny garden patch
- Shovel
- Short stakes
- String
- Tall-growing sunflower seeds
- Cheesecloth (optional)

Step by Step:

1. Late in spring, when the weather is warm, mark the rectangle in the garden.
2. Prepare the soil for your walls. Loosen it by digging a trench 1 ft. wide by 1 ft. deep (30 × 30 cm).
3. Amend soil if required to properly grow the plants.
4. Push a stake in the ground at each corner. Mark the "doorway" with stakes.
5. Tie a string to the doorway stake and run the string around the stakes, surrounding your fort. This acts as a guide to ensure you plant in straight lines.

6. Plant seeds 1 in. (2.5 cm) deep and 6 in. (15 cm) apart around the edges of the fort, excluding the doorway.

7. Water and lightly cover the seeds with cheesecloth (optional) to protect from birds and animals. Weigh edges down with dirt to keep cloth from blowing away.

8. Water the sunflower plants several times each week, preferably in the morning.

9. When the plants are 2 in. (5 cm) tall, remove the cheesecloth. Thin out the plants to 1 ft. (30 cm) apart as sunflowers get huge and need space.

10. Remove any weeds and keep the plants watered—sunflowers need plenty of moisture.

11. Create the roof when the sunflowers are approximately 6 ft. (2 m) tall by loosely tying the tops of the plants from one side of the fort to the tops of the plants from the other side of the fort all around the fort. Tie baling twine in a loop (so not to crush plants) to the stems about 1 ft. (30 cm) below the bloom and bend the stalk gently toward the flower on the opposite side of the house until the two touch. Don't tie too tight, or you will damage the sunflower stems!

12. Line the inside of your house with straw, blankets or other comfortable flooring.

13. Try making a sunflower fort in different shapes! For example, lay out a large circle in your garden, then create a maze-like path to the centre of the circle. Children can walk through the sunflower maze to reach their play space in the centre.

14. For added colour, plant climbing annuals such as nasturtiums or morning glory at the base of the sunflowers, which can serve as a trellis.

15. You can plant a variety of sunflowers that grow to different heights—the tallest will create the walls and roof of your house, the shorter sunflowers will help fill in the walls.

Monster and Mini Sunflowers:

Monster Sized, for the main supports:
- 'Kong' – to 12 ft. (3.5 m) tall
- 'Russian Mammoth' – to 10–12 ft. (3–3.5 m) with flowers 1–2 ft. (30–60 cm)

Mid Sized, for between the monster stalks and to add colour variation:
- 'Autumn Beauty' – to 5–6 ft. (1.5–1.8 m) with flowers 5 in. (13 cm)
- 'Indian Blanket' – to 5–7 ft. (1.5–2.2 m) with flowers 4–5 in. (10–13 cm)

Mini Sized, to embellish your sunflower house at knee level:
- 'Teddy Bear' – to 3 ft. (90 cm) with flowers 3–6 in. (8–15 cm)
- 'Sundance Kid' – to 1–2 ft. (30–60 cm)

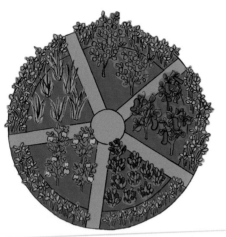

This pizza-garden plan has all the makings for a great vegetarian pizza: 'Margherita' tomatoes, 'Baby Bell' peppers, 'Genovese' basil, garlic, Italian parsley and eggplant.

Rosemary attracts beneficial pollinators and deters cabbage moths, bean beetles and carrot flies. It makes a great seasoning and the stems are useful as skewers for barbecuing.

©iStockphoto.com/Angelafoto

FUN THEMES

TREE FORTS

Tree forts are a fun and kid-friendly way to get up close and personal with fruit or nut trees. Build them on stilts and nestled in a tree canopy instead of using branches for structural support.

PIZZA GARDEN

Children can grow the fresh ingredients for pizza sauce—tomato plants, basil, rosemary and oregano, onions and peppers. Create a round bed in the garden that looks like a pizza and plant individual slices. Use brick and other walkable surfaces to act as a maintenance path, as well as defining the edges. At harvest time, buy plain pizza crust or dough, and help kids cook up a sauce using garden-fresh ingredients.

ALPHABET GARDEN

Grow an ABC garden, using vegetables that start with the first three letters of the alphabet: asparagus, butter beans, broccoli, cabbage and carrots are all good choices. Or you can spell out a child's name with vegetables: for "Joe" plant Jerusalem artichokes, okra and eggplant.

FUNKY IDEAS

Old pieces of furniture, when left out to weather, can be funky supports for climbing vegetable plants. A well-worn rocking chair would be a charming place for a growing pumpkin to ripen! A battered wooden ladder, placed strategically in the garden, is perfect for supporting climbing edible nasturtiums or fruiting gourds. Scarecrows are not only functional but can add an amusing touch to your garden that children love.

Container plantings are a simple and minimal investment to introduce children to growing food. Encourage your children to make their own and be

Inject your own personal touches into the garden to add interest, colour and another level of detail.

creative—consider a pair of colourful boots or an old toy dump truck. Almost anything that can hold soil and drains water can be used. And there are plenty of matching colourful dwarf patio edibles that will grow in them. For summer fun I use bright-coloured plastic ice buckets (adding drainage holes to them) as containers.

CHILD-FRIENDLY PLANTINGS

Edibles should always be age appropriate. For example, while tomatoes are delicious and easy to harvest, the rest of the plant is quite poisonous and toddlers may not understand the difference between eating the fruit and rest of the plant. Favourites for many children are:

- Edibles like peas, beans and squash that have large seeds little hands can plant easily.
- Quick growers like lettuce, radishes and kale.
- Sturdy plants like bush beans.
- Munchable plants like snow peas, strawberries and blueberries.
- Plants with varying textures, like prickly (squash vines) or smooth (peppers).
- Plants of different sizes—consider tall sunflowers, huge-leaved squashes and tiny-leaved thyme.
- Colourful choices like nasturtiums, sunflowers and 'Rainbow' Swiss chard.
- Fragrant herbs like basil, thyme and mint.

Allow children the freedom to plant
their own garden as they see fit.
What is messy to an adult is a
treasure trove of discovery to them.

DESIGNER TIPS

Your design approach and philosophy for a children's garden should be fun, fun, fun! Remember back to when you were a child and what you enjoyed most. And think pint-sized scale.

Leave behind adult ideas about gardening. Straight rows of immaculately tended tomatoes, peppers and corn may be your idea of the perfect garden, but are probably far from what a child finds inviting.

Start small, so the garden isn't overwhelming—a plot 3 × 3 ft. (90 × 90 cm) is enough.

Involve children in the planning, and then follow the child's lead. If she'd rather play in the dirt or look at bugs than pull weeds, that's okay!

Give children separate spaces to garden just for themselves, and let them plant and tend it in their own way. Be prepared for a garden that might be dug up, replanted, reworked and changed as children explore new ideas.

Fill the space with flexible elements such as fun containers, pebbles, bark and seeds, and add a safe water element to encourage play. Even a worm composter can be a fascinating element that encourages responsibility.

Keep safety in mind: consider soil contaminants and poisonous plants. Use only safe organic materials.

Keep chore sessions short. Make a game of weeding, but limit it to five minutes.

Use child-sized tools for planting and digging. Even spoons will work well when held with tiny fingers.

Help children succeed by sharing your gardening know-how. Find those teachable moments as they happen—admire bugs, worms and birds, all as much a part of the edible garden system as the plants.

Help the garden succeed by choosing the right site and adding the appropriate soil amendments along with mulch to keep down weeds.

By having a vested interest in gardening, children:

- Learn about nurturing and what it takes to keep something alive. A garden teaches children to respect even the smallest life such as a plant seedling.
- Are likely to eat more vegetables. Empower the children in your life by encouraging them to choose vegetable seeds, and plant, tend, harvest and eat their crops. Homegrown edibles taste a lot better than commercially produced food.
- Actually learn where vegetables come from, how they grow and what they look like—and they start to understand how interconnected everything is in nature, including themselves.
- Connect with you—gardening is an activity that invites involvement as you teach children how to plant and care for their seedlings.
- Eat better and get more exercise, teaching them lifelong good-health habits.

Edible roofs can be as simple as wooden planters
on top of structures.

©Senga Lindsay

THE EDIBLE ROOFTOP

No ground to grow your edibles? Think up—onto your rooftop! If you don't want to allocate valuable real estate to creating an edible garden but still want the pleasure of growing vegetables and fruits, a green roof may be the solution for you.

Although green roofs have been around for centuries, the concept was popularized in Germany about 50 years ago. A green roof is simply a living plant cover on a structure. The most common example seen today is an extensive roof where sedums or grass are grown in soils 4–6 in. (10–15 cm) deep. Now with urban agriculture gaining momentum, a new type of roof garden has emerged—the edible kind! With less than 1 ft. (30 cm) of soil, you can grow most vegetables, herbs and even some fruits on top of your house, shed or garage.

©Sergh Lindsay

A Beams and posts are reinforced to municipal green-roof code and to support additional weight

B Waterproof roof with drainage layer encourages drainage

C Walkways 2 ft. (60 cm) wide allow for safe movement and bed access

D Lightweight green-roof soil reduces the load on the roof structure

E Raised planter beds with open bottoms lined with filter fabric allow for drainage

F Guardrails line the perimeter of the roof

G Trellising on the north side supports vertical planting

H Beehives boost pollination

I Good drainage system

J Rain barrels collect water runoff from roof drains

This rooftop vegetable garden is watered using rain collected from barrels.

THE PLAN

Roof Dimensions: 28 × 24 ft. (8.5 × 7.2 m) 672 sq. ft. (62 sq. m)

Total Area of Edibles: 250 sq. ft. (23 sq. m) of raised beds, 120 sq. ft. (11 sq. m) vertically

DESIGNER NOTES

The garage structure was upgraded and raised planters of various sizes were added. Using the square foot method (see page 119) and five raised planters (total of 228 sq. ft./21 sq. m) filled with only 10 in. (25 cm) of lightweight green-roof soil, I harvested fresh produce through most of the year. The costs to install my rooftop garden were as follows:

- Lumber, filter cloth and hardware: $500
- Structural reinforcement: $300
- Green-roof soil (8 cu. yd. or 6 cu. m @ $65/cu. yd.): $520
- Seeds: $100 or less (and I have enough seed for the next 5 years!)
- Labour: Free (I did it myself!)

My edible green roof is bare bones in design and located on top of a two-car garage.

©Serga Lindsey

Did you know? The advantages of using your rooftop for your edible garden are numerous including:

1. A controlled and sanitary environment that means less disease, weeds and pest issues.

2. Less chance of marauders (i.e., rabbits and, for me, bears!) raiding the garden.

3. The freeing up of valuable outdoor real estate on the ground.

4. Less flooding, as the rooftop garden captures the rainwater, with less flowing into the overloaded city sewers. For a truly efficient system, attach rain barrels to your drains below to capture water for use in your garden.

5. An excellent source of pollen and nectar for butterflies and bees.

6. Increased oxygenation—living plants add oxygen and absorb carbon dioxide.

DESIGN ELEMENTS

BEFORE YOU BEGIN

There are a few considerations to take into account before diving into construction—and they are important ones.

LOAD ON THE ROOF

The first step is to evaluate your roof's loading capacity. This is the amount of weight your roof structure can support and includes everything: planter boxes, soil (when wet), possible water storage, weight of crops at maturity, equipment and such temporary loads as people and snow. This may be your biggest expense and will determine whether you are willing to pursue an edible roof or not. Working with a structural engineer is a must!

Contact a structural engineer and discuss what you intend to design; for this, a plan of your garden is required. The engineer will evaluate the possibility of carrying out the project, what it would take in terms of reinforcement, and the influence of obstacles (vents, chimneys, etc.) and/or possibility of eliminating or moving them.

MUNICIPAL REGULATIONS

Review your municipality's regulations. Architects or building designers can often assist you in interpreting building-code requirements for green roofs.

SUN AND WIND EXPOSURE

Consider sun and wind exposure. Edible plants require a minimum of six hours, with heliophilous plants such as tomatoes needing at least ten. Study your patterns and hours of sunlight and note adjacent buildings that may create additional shadows. Wind is often stronger at rooftop heights than on ground level and can cause

Build planters to hold soil, keeping the bottoms open to allow for drainage.

©Serge Lirdsay

Line your boxes with filter fabric to hold the soil.

©Serge Lirdsay

serious damage to plants. Structural windbreakers may need to be designed in conjunction with the building frame and they must be able to withstand wind loads.

ADDITIONAL CONSIDERATIONS

Depending on how elaborate you want to go, additional considerations may be:

- Storage or areas for composting
- Rainwater collection system—possibly from adjacent roofs with storage on garden roof
- Electricity for running power tools and equipment
- General security and lock off to limit access

MY EDIBLE GREEN ROOF

My edible green roof is bare bones in design and located on top of a two-car garage. I wanted maximum vegetable production but did not want to use up my at-grade outdoor dining areas or wildlife gardens. I also wanted to keep a couple of beehives for honey and pollination but did not want ninety thousand bees buzzing around at ground level.

CREATING AN EDIBLE GREEN ROOF ON A GARAGE

PREPARE YOUR ROOF STRUCTURALLY

Ensure it meets municipal building and safety requirements for a green roof. Also, check that your roof membrane can support walking and planters— you don't want to risk a leak! Flat roofs are best.

BUILD PLANTERS TO HOLD SOIL

Here I use 2 × 4 fir on sleepers, allowing for 10 in. (25 cm) of soil. Gravel on the roof encourages drainage, which is an absolute must, so check that your roof drains properly!

Add lightweight green-roof soil.

©Sonya Lindsay

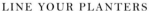

©Sonya Lindsay

Adding bees is a great way to increase food production through pollination, plus you get honey!

LINE YOUR PLANTERS

Use weed block to contain soil while allowing drainage.

ADD GREEN-ROOF SOIL

Lightweight soil specific for green roofs is placed in raised planters (soil weight: 75 lb. per sq. ft. or approx. 300 kg per sq. m). A bonus is that this mix starts out with no weed seeds.

PLANT VEGETABLES, HERBS AND FRUIT

Swiss chard, watermelon, iceberg and assorted leaf lettuce, vine and cherry tomatoes, zucchini, cucumbers, peppers and everbearing strawberries are my favourites.

Tip: To grow vegetables that require more soil depth without committing to larger roof loads, use deeper containers in strategic spots (over your roof beam or posts). Always check with your structural engineer on any roof-load issues.

THE EDIBLE WALL

For those of us with limited space, edible walls are a creative and beautiful alternative. Just imagine harvesting herbs, strawberries, lettuce or tomatoes from the side of your garage or fence. The famed New York chef Mario Batali loves the idea of edible walls and has installed them on both his restaurants in Los Angeles. With similar advantages to a rooftop garden, they can also help to insulate a building and have incredible ornamental appeal.

©judywhite/GardenPhotos.com

Edible walls can be turned into focal pieces for the garden.

A A free-standing panel system works as a screen to provide privacy

B The trellised container garden multi-tasks as a striking landscape focal point

C The panel system integrates into the existing wall and becomes part of this fireplace feature

D Planting trench contains overflow from the living-wall irrigation system

E A barbecue adjacent to the edible wall allows for easy-reach harvesting and cooking

The panel system is a series of planted trays that are fastened vertically to walls or a frame.

Edible walls make stylish additions to any building façade.

TYPES OF EDIBLE WALLS

PANEL SYSTEM

This is a system that consists of a wall panel or modular box filled with soil and planted up. The panel or box is covered with fabric or metal to contain the soil and punctured with openings to allow the plants to grow through. The panels or boxes can be interconnected and hung vertically—usually on an existing wall. The standard wall panel measures 2 ft. (60 cm) square by about 4 in. (10 cm) deep.

Nutrients are primarily distributed through an irrigation system that cycles water from the top of the system down. Irrigation typically consists of an 8-mm dripline that weaves in between the panels. This can be fully automatic and comes complete with a rain sensor to prevent water waste.

The soil used should be a blend similar to that for green roofs—lighter in weight than traditional soil (which may be too heavy to be supported by an existing wall).

An edible wall can accommodate a huge variety of crops, from perennials like herbs and strawberries to tomatoes, eggplants and peppers to vines like peas. Lettuce is a popular choice as it is quick to grow and available in a wide colour palette. While plants can be sown from seed, best results are usually achieved using plugs or small starts that won't fall through the slots.

With additional framework, edible walls can be converted into adventurous structures. For example, the "Eat House" (page 51) is not only a "building" but a garden to eat, smell, taste, seed, weed and harvest! It consists of a modular system of recycled vegetable crates from the agricultural industry, in combination with a scaffold structure that can be relocated and reused if desired.

Edible walls can be free-standing or attached to building structures.

Pocket systems are simply felt pouches that hold water, soil and edibles.

CONTAINER OR TRELLIS SYSTEM

Plants are grown in containers at the base of a wall and encouraged to climb up trellises or other supports. Irrigation driplines are used in the containers to maintain moisture levels.

POCKET SYSTEMS

Plants are grown in pockets attached to a waterproof backing connected to a rigid structure. The plants are kept moist by a drip system; often these pockets are made of felt that is kept continuously wet through irrigation.

Panels structurally supported as a free-standing wall can make great privacy screens or act as a fence around your property.

THE A-FRAME WALL

This is a perfect alternative for those who do not have walls or a structure to support their vertical gardens. This prefabricated A-frame system is made out of durable food-grade aluminum panels and can grow 96 sq. ft. (9 sq. m) of food while utilizing only 32 sq. ft. (3 sq. m) of horizontal space. Mounted on wheels, it can be relocated to maximize exposure to the sun or located wherever there is unused space. Manual irrigation is accomplished by adding water to the drip reservoir at the top of the unit, or optional metered and automatic irrigation is also available. Or, with a bit of ingenuity you can create your own structure and fasten the panels to it.

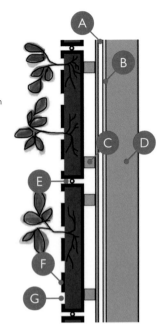

PANEL SYSTEM

A Vertical channel

B Waterproofing

C Horizontal purlin

D Structure

E Dripline

F Wall panel with growing medium

G Perforations

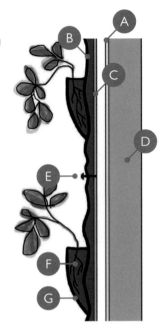

FELT POCKET SYSTEM

A Waterproofing

B Felt layer

C Backing

D Structure

E Tie

F Growing medium

G Pocket

ADDITIONAL CONSIDERATIONS

COST

Edible walls cost $50 to $200 per square foot, depending on how elaborate your wall or detailing is.

PERMISSIONS AND REGULATIONS

It is very important for apartment dwellers to obtain permission from their strata or tenants' association. Always check with local jurisdiction to ensure you are complying with building codes, and double-check that any insurance coverage is not affected by the addition of a living wall.

STRUCTURAL CONCERNS

A living wall is typically attached to an existing structure, adding significant weight or "load." Consult an architect before starting to evaluate your course of action. It may be that structural and building-envelope engineers will need to be involved.

Also, ensure your wall is waterproofed correctly, as these systems hold a lot of moisture (wet soil). Whether by hand or automatic, your irrigation system is bound to send overspray onto the building envelope.

DRAINAGE AND OVERFLOW

Most systems are free draining by design. Catch basins can be added at the base of the wall for capturing excess rain and irrigation runoff, however, the system may overflow at times. Ensure overflow will drain properly or be redirected to a secondary system. This is particularly important for apartment dwellers using decks that may not be properly designed to drain water—in short, you may end up soaking your neighbour below!

IRRIGATION

Whether you hand water or install an irrigation system, access to a nearby water supply is a must.

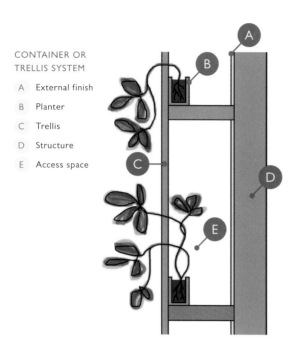

CONTAINER OR
TRELLIS SYSTEM

A   External finish

B   Planter

C   Trellis

D   Structure

E   Access space

Portable walls can be moved to follow the sun or weather patterns.

SUN AND WIND EXPOSURE

Edibles require a minimum of six hours of sunlight, so orient your living walls to receive maximum sunshine. But remember that the higher up you go on a balcony or rooftop the more extreme the effects of sun and wind. Therefore, observe your microclimates and exposures and angle your walls away from full and direct sun and wind if you feel the plants are in danger of suffering from overexposure.

MAINTENANCE

While general maintenance—pruning, fertilizing, harvesting and pest/disease control—is similar to any garden, soil replenishment and moisture monitoring are bigger issues when you are growing an edible wall:

SOIL REPLENISHMENT

Over the course of many seasons, plants will deplete the soil and it will need replacing. To slow down this process, cut the spent vegetation off at root level and allow the roots to decompose and become organic material.

MOISTURE MONITORING

The driplines typically used between panels can clog or malfunction. Ensure your irrigation system is functioning properly by routinely checking that the soil is adequately moist.

Unlike traditional edible garden or agriculture
production, permaculture is a way of assembling
all the elements in your landscape for the benefit
of life in its many forms.

THE PERMACULTURE GARDEN

Although the concept isn't new, permaculture is a current "catch phrase" and trend in edible landscaping. Developed in the 1970s in Australia by Bill Mollison, it is a cohesive approach to designing a productive ecosystem reminiscent of nature.

The key to designing a successful and beautiful permaculture garden is to ensure all the elements in your garden connect to one another in a beneficial way. Think of the multitude of uses for each component in your garden. For example, a fruit tree can provide food, ornamental value and shade, as well as serve as a wildlife habitat and windbreak. In a good permaculture design, every aspect of a garden supports another, and tedious tasks such as weeding and watering are often minimized.

While permaculture principles work on every scale—from balcony spaces to large farms—our design focuses on a backyard with a functional yet aesthetically pleasing layout. Outdoor living areas adjacent to the house front onto a water feature fed by rainwater that drains off the roof and sustains edible plants like taro root, water spinach and watercress. The patio is framed by a trellis supporting grapevines that provide shade during hot days and fruit in the fall. Often-used herbs and salad crops grow adjacent to the patio to allow easy access for daily harvesting. An orchard of columnar dwarf fruit trees provides architectural structure as well as food, and is underplanted with a living mulch of weed-suppressing perennial strawberries punctuated on the corners by edible flowers and companion plants. The orchard also provides partial screening of back-of-house operations such as a functional vegetable garden, chicken coop, storage shed and compost bin. The yard is bordered by fruit-bearing raspberries and currants, underplanted with quick-growing cool crops that require shade during summer months.

A Stacking and interplanting maximizes edible production

B Multi-tasking drainage systems provide aquaculture opportunities

C Walls and vertical elements provide opportunities for growing vining edibles

D Beehives are positioned off ground to avoid conflict with human activities

E Overhead structures support edible vines and provide shade for seating areas

F Zone 1 higher-maintenance and frequently used edibles are located closer to the house

G Dwarf fruit trees allow for easy reaching

H Outbuildings provide storage for tools and more

I An area for composting and "back of the house" activities is tucked into a corner

J Zone 2–3 edible gardens are relegated to the rear of the garden

K Hard-surface pathways a minimum of 2 ft. (60 cm) wide allow for easy access to planters and wheelbarrow passage

L Animal husbandry is incorporated wherever possible

THE PLAN

Yard Dimensions: 50 × 46 ft. (15 × 14 m)
Total Area of Edibles: 1,185 sq. ft. (110 sq. m)

DESIGN ELEMENTS

CREATE ZONES

Based on how frequently you visit each particular area, define zones in your permaculture design. Start with your house as Zone 0.

ZONE 1

Everything that needs a lot of attention should be considered Zone 1. This includes areas where you spend a lot of time, along with gardens that require daily attention, such as those with seedlings that need regular watering, herbs for kitchen use, salad vegetables and even your compost bin.

ZONE 2

Those areas in Zone 2 also require regular attention, but less so—you shouldn't need to check or use them daily. Often fully irrigated and mulched to suppress weeds and retain soil moisture, they usually contain smaller fruit trees, shrubs and trellised fruit. Vegetables that take a long time to mature and are only picked once or twice (think cauliflower and bulb onions) also belong in Zone 2, along with perennial or self-seeding herbs that are not used daily.

ZONES 3, 4, 5

Depending on how much land you are working with, you may not have much room for the remaining zones. Zone 3 features large fruit or nut trees, and Zones 4 and 5 usually include wilder areas that require little or no management.

This simple but elegant composition of edible red-veined sorrel (left) and society garlic (right) is an example of a guild of plants—they both love water. This bowl also provides a steady water source for bees.

DIVERSIFY, DIVERSIFY, DIVERSIFY

Mix and match as many different plants as possible. And let go of the idea that a food or vegetable patch has to be separate from the rest of the garden, that plants must grow in rows or allotted beds. Different plants have varying nutrient requirements—put the right ones together and you can fit many into a small space without depleting the soil. In nature—whether forest, meadow or wetland—there is no single area that has only one plant species. Diversity can confuse insect predators (as one favourite food source doesn't stand out), deter disease (as it can't spread easily through related plants), and extend the harvest season (with a mix of early- and late-ripening edibles). Look at how plants work together in nature, and work to mimic that design in your garden.

USE AS LITTLE SPACE AS POSSIBLE

Even if you have a very small garden, use it efficiently so you can not only grow a year-round supply of fresh herbs and vegetables but also have space for wildlife. You can minimize the space you use and maximize your harvest by using techniques like stacking and growing in guilds.

STACK 'EM

Stacking means planting different species together to make maximum use of vertical space. A classic example involves sweet corn, beans and cucumbers. The tall corn serves as a trellis for the beans, while the prickly-leaved squash ramble around the corn, discouraging racoons from harvesting the cobs. Three crops grow in the space of one, all supporting each other in varying ways.

A low-lying muddy spot is the perfect location for a pond and moisture-loving edibles like watercress.

Shallow-rooted edibles such as strawberries can grow and thrive in even 3 in. (7.5 cm) of soil.

Rain harvesting is a system that channels water from a roof into a storage tank via an arrangement of gutters and pipes.

GROWING IN GUILDS

A guild is a grouping together of species that exploit the same resources, often in related ways. Some plants may be grown for food production, some to attract beneficial insects, and others to repel harmful insects. For more on this, reference the companion planting chart (see page 61).

TURN A DISADVANTAGE INTO AN ADVANTAGE

Got a low-lying spot at the bottom end of your garden that is always muddy? This may be the perfect location for a pond and a place for growing water-loving edibles like watercress. By looking at a problem as a possible solution you can change your site challenges to advantages. And in the case of a pond, you would be providing one of the most valuable resources in nature—water—which would attract wildlife including beneficial insects. My honeybees require a tremendous amount of water during the summer to maintain a hive and produce honey; once they have found a water source, they rely on it from that point forward.

ON EDGE

In nature, edges between woodlands and meadows are amongst the most dynamic ecosystems. Called "the edge effect," the area where contrasting environments connect is intensely dynamic and productive. This also pertains to gardens where contrasting elements meet, so take advantage of this. To maximize edges, create ponds with wavy undulating shorelines rather than a simple circle, or design a spiraling herb garden as opposed to square.

Put up mason bee houses to attract these native pollinators.

ADDITIONAL CONSIDERATIONS

INCLUDE ANIMALS

In permaculture, animals are often incorporated into the site design. More and more municipalities are allowing chickens in backyards. Apart from the obvious—fresh eggs!—chickens produce fertilizer for the garden and help with weed and insect control. Chicken coops can be designed to be mobile and placed on vegetable beds between plantings. The chickens go to work cleaning up residual weeds and insects and leave their droppings as fertilizer. Simply rake up those droppings and scoop them into your compost—it's considered safest to ensure chicken manure is well composted before being dug into your vegetable garden.

SUPPORT BEES

Bee-keeping is another way to benefit a garden. Responsible for pollinating roughly 75 percent of our food crops, the hardworking bees also provide honey, wax and propolis. Or if this seems like too much to take on, at least consider putting up a mason bee house in a protected area, possibly under the eaves of your house. Active in cold wet weather when honeybees are dormant, these solitary bees are similar in appearance to common houseflies and vital for the pollination of early crops.

COLLECT RAINWATER

For those with metal or other non-toxic roofing materials, use rain barrels to harvest rainwater from your roof for your gardens and you will be literally saving this precious resource from going down the drain.

Chicken tractors can be moved around your garden beds—the chickens will clean up your harvested bed and deposit fertilizer!

Add honeybees to dramatically increase your harvest.

COMPANION PLANTING GUIDE

Plant	Beneficial Companions	Bad Companions
Apples	Chives, nasturtiums	Potatoes (host blights)
Basil	Tomatoes, lettuce, salad leaves	Cabbage, cauliflower, pumpkins
Beans	Potatoes, carrots, cauliflower, cabbage, celeriac	Onions, garlic, leeks
Brassicas (cabbage family)	Potatoes, celery (do not compete for food)	Tomatoes, strawberries (compete for food)
Carrots	Peas, chives, tomatoes, lettuce, radish, marigolds	Dill
Celery	Leeks, tomatoes, brassicas	Silver beet hosts rust
Chives	Carrots, parsley	Peas, beans
Cucumber	Peas, radishes	Potatoes, aromatic herbs (i.e. mint)
French marigold	Tomatoes, carrots	None
Leeks	Onions, celery, carrots	Beans
Lettuce	Carrots, radish, strawberries, cucumber	None
Onions	Strawberries, lettuce	Peas, beans
Parsley	Carrots, tomatoes	Onions, garlic, leeks
Peas	Carrots, beans, cucumbers	Onion, garlic, leeks
Pumpkin	Corn	Potatoes
Radish	Carrots, peas, lettuce, cucumber	None
Strawberries	Lettuce, onion, garlic	Eggplant
Squash, zucchini	Nasturtiums	Potatoes, aromatic herbs (i.e. mint)
Tomatoes	Chives, onion, parsley	Potatoes, kohlrabi, broccoli, cabbage

Repetitive geometric themes accentuated by ornamental plants make the potager garden elaborate yet highly functional.

THE POTAGER GARDEN

Initially developed by French monks, the potager kitchen garden (pronounced poe-ta-zhay) became popular in the 16th century in France. The potager concept ranged from large chateaus where they were elaborate, high maintenance and indicative of the wealth of the occupants, to the common farmyard where they could still be showy but were usually more relaxed in form. And today in France you will find that understated elegance is still in vogue for potager design.

Unlike the traditional kitchen garden, which is highly practical with edibles grown in long parallel rows, in France the potager evolved into something more stylized and formal. Although they served the same purpose—that of producing food—the potager garden's layout and plantings were much more elaborate, using themes of geometry and repetition of vegetable beds accentuated by ornamental or flowering plants. Often low-clipped boxwood hedges were used as garden borders or weaved into patterns within each individual bed. Permanent pathways in a variety of decorative or durable materials were used to accent and access these beds.

Sized for the urban gardener, this potager garden is still large enough to provide a family with daily fresh vegetables, and is accented by fruit and flowers.

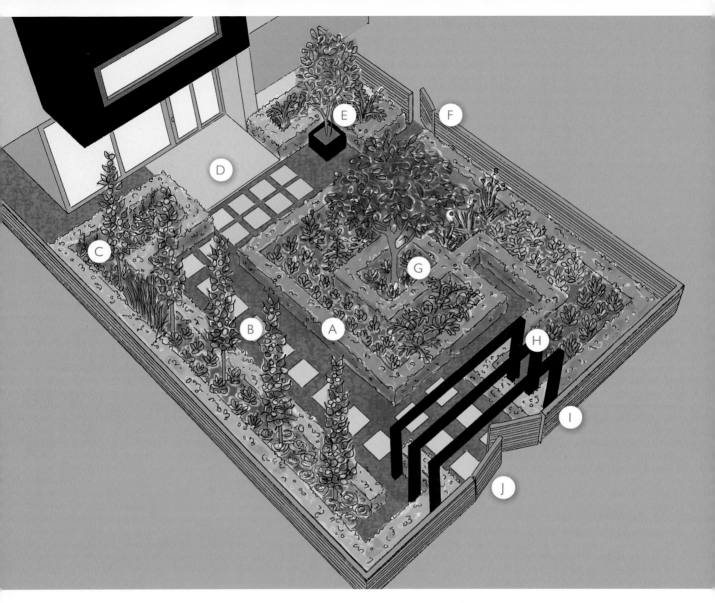

A   Boxwood or other evergreen hedging creates permanent "bones" in the garden and adds a sense of formality

B   Oversized hard-surface pathways (a minimum of 3 ft./90 cm wide) add presence and ornamentation as well as functionality to the garden

C   Columnar fruit trees planted in a row add rhythm and formality to a landscape design

D   A wide landing gives emphasis to the entrance

E   Planter pots provide additional ornamentation and focal points to the garden

F   A gate and path ensure access to the rest of the property

G   Focal points in the garden add curb appeal; consider specimen trees, special plantings or sculptural elements

H   An arbour marks the entrance to the potager garden and provides support for climbing edibles

I   Fencing or walls offer enclosure and also provide opportunities for climbing edibles or espaliers

J   A gate adds ornamentation and marks the entry sequence to the front yard and door

Create seasonal displays or vegetable themes in each section of the potager garden.

THE PLAN

Yard Dimensions: 33 × 43 ft. (10 × 13 m)
Total Area of Edibles: 235 sq. ft. (22 sq. m)

DESIGNER NOTE

Most front yards are underutilized and can be non-descript. This potager garden located in the front yard acts not only as a stylish entrance to the front door but supplies fresh produce and flowers throughout the growing season. An entrance arbour and perimeter fence encapsulates the garden, which features fruit trees, evergreen boxwood hedging and an architectural walkway—all permanent elements that provide structure and interest year round.

> Did you know? "Potager" translated means a vegetable stew or soup.

DESIGN ELEMENTS

BED LAYOUT

Potager gardens are all about the ebb and flow of the seasons—whether for flower or food. Whatever your design, divide your potager into sections, dedicating each to a specific seasonal vegetable.

Whatever season you start in, plant about two-thirds of your potager plots, leaving one-third free to be planted for later vegetables. Your potager will slowly move through the seasons as your vegetables mature and are harvested, each plot tilled and replanted. For those of us who can't afford the luxury of a large estate, think of smaller beds as per the design shown. By maintaining the 4-ft. (1.2-m) bed-width rule (for accessing vegetable beds from both sides) plant blocks of single edibles or flowers in long rows (a minimum 10 ft./3 m if possible) for maximum colour and texture. Access paths should be a minimum of 2 ft. (.6 m) wide.

Potager gardens can also be divided geometrically into many small square, rectangular or triangular beds, each bordered by a low hedge and separated by immaculate pathways.

> Tip: Remember to position your tallest plants in the northern portion of your potager.

Permanent elements such as arbours, trees or hedging add interest all year round.

WALLS

Bordering of the garden can be created with walls, fences or thick hedges, and heights can vary depending on your needs. Some enclosures such as open fencing can double as support for espaliered fruit trees or tall plantings. Stone or brick walls are often used for protection from both critters and brisk winds. Walls also create microclimates—south walls retain more heat and delicate plants can be lined up against them.

PATHWAYS

Pathways not only allow access to your beds but are decorative features in themselves, adding to the aesthetic of the whole garden. Use materials such as coarse mulch, gravel, bricks, cement or even bare soil. A minimum of 2 ft. (60 cm) is required for access to each bed but you may want to broaden and formalize pathways depending on how ornamental you wish your garden to become. A width of 3–6 ft. (90–180 cm) is very much in keeping with the grander design of a potager.

EDGINGS

Typically, low boxwood hedges are used for edging potager beds and are clipped into geometric hard edges. Boxwood's evergreen leaves ensure the garden still looks good in the winter when the beds are bare. If you wish, flowering annuals such as nasturtiums or marigolds, or ornamental cabbage or herbs, can be also be used for edging, as they echo seasonal plantings and add a riot of colour. And borders need not be limited to plants. Hard materials such as wood, stone and basket-weave fences are just a few of the many alternatives. The choice comes down to your style preference and how much time you want to devote to maintaining your edging. Clipped boxwood hedging admittedly takes time to maintain if you want it to look elegant.

STRUCTURES

The bones of your potager should be vertical, consisting of arbours, small trees (espaliered forms are popular) or garden ornamentation. The vertical component can also be expressed with walls, gates and even terraces, and further defines the personal style of your space. Rhythmic repetition of elements adds interest and reinforces the structure and formality of your garden.

COLOURFUL AND MIXED PLANTINGS

Contrasting colours and edibles are often mixed with flowering annuals, perennials and herbs. Boxwood or formal edgings hold back what can be neatly confined rows of plantings or a more chaotic and romantic mixture of vegetables and flowers.

Use perennial favourite herbs such as lavender, rosemary, thyme, oregano, marjoram and tarragon. Other classic plantings for a potager might include strawberries, melons, annual herbs, espaliered fruit trees and, of course, coloured vegetables such as leaf lettuces, which can provide a rotating seasonal display of colour.

Tip: Use parsley for your edging. Parsley is one of the top herbs used in cooking and you can never get enough of it.

A FOCAL POINT

Consider a small tree, garden ornament, urn or statuary as a focal point. Also impressive is an artichoke plant, which renews itself year after year, or perhaps a sundial, bird bath, obelisk or planted arbour.

OUTBUILDINGS

Small buildings or a potting shed allow you to keep all your tools, seeds and spare equipment close at hand yet out of sight. Dress up the façade of your building and locate it on an axis in your garden to create a focal point. Ornately designed greenhouses can also serve this purpose.

Wood, stone and basket-weave fences are just a few of the many alternatives for edging the potager garden.

Add drama to a potager garden with a mix of colourful flowers and edibles.

When growing on public land, be prepared to share
with the neighbours!

©Gracedesigns in California

THE EDIBLE STREET GARDEN

The edible boulevard or street garden has been in existence since the 1950s in such countries as Australia where it is called "verge" or "kerbside gardening." Most commonly, boulevard gardens involve the strips of land between the public sidewalk and road. Planting up this space is a great way to grow food while also beautifying your streetscape and inspiring your neighbours.

In North America this idea is only recently capturing the public imagination and the number of these gardens is rapidly accelerating. As a result many cities are currently implementing guidelines that take into consideration the interface between the boulevard garden and automobile and pedestrian traffic.

©Songa Lindsay

Planting up your boulevard is a great way to grow food while also beautifying your streetscape and inspiring neighbours.

A   Periodic hard-surface access allows for the passage of pedestrians from the sidewalk to parked cars—a minimum width of 4 ft. (120 cm) allows for wheelchairs, walking aids and strollers

B   Leaf lettuces and other leafy crops are planted away from road curbs and car influences

C   Where edible crops are adjacent to curbs, raised wooden planters 18 in. (45 cm) high will protect them from contaminants

D   Dwarf or columnar fruit trees save space and do not encroach on parked cars or pedestrian traffic

E   Where allowable, raised containers within planters maximize space and accommodate trailing edibles—but they should not exceed 3 ft. (1 m) in height

F   A 1-ft. (30-cm) setback from the road curb allows the doors of parked cars to be opened and enables people to manoeuvre

G   At critical junctions or corners, low edibles are planted so as not to impede vision

THE PLAN

Boulevard Dimensions:

Concept #1 Street Boulevard: 33 × 6 ft. (10 × 1.8 m)

Concept #2 Traffic Bulge Boulevard: 33 × 14
   ft. (10 × 4.3 m)

Total Area of Edibles: 193 sq. ft. (18 sq. m) or 460 sq.
   ft. (43 sq. m) respectively

Average Street Boulevard: 193 sq. ft. (18 sq. m)

Traffic Bulge Boulevard: 246 sq. ft. (23 sq. m)

Ideally your boulevard garden will look vibrant all year long.

©Sanga Linkang

DESIGNER NOTE

While you can get away with a less than perfect "look"
in your own backyard, edible gardening on the public
street requires an aesthetic that will be pleasing to the
public. Therefore, additional design and maintenance
considerations should be taken seriously. This includes
everything from proper construction, use of materials
for walks and planter beds, to garden layouts that
allow easy access for pedestrians. As well, impeccable
upkeep and healthy-looking plantings are the key to
winning over your neighbours and passersby. Care
for your garden beds should include regular watering,
mulching, composting, disease and pest control
and pruning of trees and shrubs to avoid impeding
pedestrians or cars.

Tip: Start small with a limited area until you are fairly sure
the public will accept your boulevard conversion.

DESIGN ELEMENTS

BEFORE YOU BEGIN

Although you may consider a boulevard planting to be
an extension of your home garden in planting terms,
it is not in legal terms. As you are working with public
land, there is no mechanism to stop passersby from
helping themselves. Be prepared to lose some of your
harvest and possibly the occasional plant. This may
not be the place for desirable choices such as young
fruit trees or expensive shrubs. Stick with plants you
can bear to lose, and many gardeners who grow edible
crops in boulevard plots do so with a sharing spirit.

Tip: To minimize damage, place a little sign suggesting
people enjoy edible leaves or fruit when ripe but not pick
the entire plant.

CONSULT LOCAL AUTHORITIES

Anything beyond your property is considered public
so check your property survey and measure on-site
to locate where your private yard ends and the public
realm begins. Cities have established standards for
maintenance and construction of public landscapes.
that have traditionally taken the form of street
trees and lawn.

Before you put a shovel in the ground, consult
with the governing authority in your neighbourhood
for their policies. Often you will be required to follow
a set of guidelines for "Non-Standard Boulevard
Treatments" and sign or register your edible garden.
Bear in mind that although permission may be
granted, usually the city reserves the right to require,
under certain circumstances, that the boulevard be
returned to its original standard at your expense. Also

A   Trees are pruned so that they are not obstacles to pedestrians or cars

B   If accessible on all sides, beds are no more than 4 ft. (120 cm) wide to avoid the trampling of crops and soil

C   Leaf lettuce and other leafy crops are planted away from road curbs and car influences

D   Periodic hard-surface access allows for the passage of pedestrians from the sidewalk to parked cars—a minimum width of 4 ft. (120 cm) allows for wheelchairs, walking aids and strollers

E   Where allowable, raised wooden planters 18 in. (45 cm) high will protect edible crops adjacent to curbs from contaminants

F   A 1-ft. (30-cm) setback from the road curb allows the doors of parked cars to be opened and enables people to manoeuvre

G   Any elements added should be easily removable if required by city authorities remember that in the event of emergency works (i.e., a ruptured line or the road is widened) the city may need to disturb or remove your garden without being obligated to reinstate it.

LOCATE ALL SERVICES

It is vital from both a legal and safety standpoint that you establish where any underground services are located prior to beginning your boulevard garden. Make sure you know the location of all gas, phone, hydro, cable and other lines prior to commencing any work. Often they are buried only 3 ft. (90 cm) deep or shallower. Tree-root balls are large—often needing to be placed at depths of 3 ft. (90 cm) or more—so it's entirely possible that you could hit a line while digging the hole. Also, check with city road engineers to confirm whether you are able to plant trees and what distance to offset root balls from the lines.

KEEP SERVICES CLEAR

Above-ground services such as fire hydrants, manholes and valves will need to remain visually clear and easily accessible for maintenance. This also includes overhead lines such as electrical and telephone. Trees should be selected so mature height does not conflict with overhead lines. Guides are often available from your local utility that list the maximum tree heights allowable.

CONSTRUCTION OF PERMANENT ELEMENTS

Any permanent fixture should be investigated in detail with city authorities prior to installation.

SET BACK TREES

Plants grow. Larger plants and trees will need to be set back from road intersections, traffic lights and signs. When in doubt, check with city road engineers who will have offset recommendations.

The blur between public and private space can be dazzling instead of dreary.

SET BACK PLANTER BEDS

Set back beds from sidewalks, road curbs and adjacent parking spaces a minimum of 1 ft. (30 cm) to allow the doors of parked cars to open and people to manoeuvre in and out easily without potential tripping hazards.

PEDESTRIAN OPENINGS

Planter beds should also provide openings to allow pedestrians to move across the street and get to and from parked cars. A width of 4 ft. (120 cm) will allow people to manoeuvre a wheelchair, pram or walking aid between the sidewalk and the curb.

PLANTING

Often (but not always) authorities will not object to your building raised garden beds on boulevards if set back from roads and walks, so it is best to check for guidelines. In addition to being one of the easiest ways to contain and tidy up the edible garden, raised beds are also a great way to protect food crops from the contamination that may be prevalent in high-traffic boulevards. For example, established boulevard soil may be on the receiving end of water draining from the street or subjected to prolonged car exhaust. Contaminants from these sources may make their way from the soil into the roots of your vegetable crops.

©iStockphoto.com/danolinglen

A good choice for the shady garden, Swiss chard is a designer's, horticulturalist's and chef's dream. In terms of pests and diseases, very little can go wrong with this vigorous "cut-and-come-again" plant. Vibrant white, red, yellow and even purple stalks have been bred into a wide variety of cultivars that you can use to accent your ornamental containers, flower border or that special culinary dish.

And if the boulevard has been in existence for years, the soil is likely compacted and low in nutrients. If it supports sod it is probably less than 8 in. (20 cm) deep.

Creating raised beds approximately 18 in. (45 cm) high; lining them with a 4-in. (10-cm) layer of drainage rock and backfilling with good composted soil will not only mitigate these potential concerns but will create a good base for healthy plants. And edges are a great way to keep mulch and soils from eroding from planter beds and being washed into the gutter and down the storm drains.

Construction materials should be clean and simple, like untreated wood or metal (without sharp edges), and keep an orderly design aesthetic that is fitting with the neighbourhood. Cities always retain the right to remove your gardens so you don't want to spend a fortune on materials. Irrigation systems and fencing will likely be rejected. Likewise with hard mulching such as pea gravel or small rocks that vandals can use as projectiles.

DRAINAGE

Garden beds should maintain positive drainage (no pooling). Be aware that piling soil too high against curbs and sidewalks can cause soil to erode and wash into streets and sidewalks.

PLANT AND TREE SELECTION

In gardens located near intersections, tall plants may be a visual impediment to drivers. Check with your municipality for guidelines on planting heights and tree setbacks. And avoid trees that have invasive roots that could lift up curbs and walkways and create tripping hazards, or damage buried utilities. Also, do not plant trees that will drop nuts or slippery fruits onto the sidewalk or parked cars. For those wishing for fruit in their gardens, columnar apple trees may be ideal.

Avoid leafy crops such as lettuce, which can be more sensitive to picking up contaminants that may wash into soil from the street. Or plant leafy greens in raised beds to mitigate this. Hardy plants for streetscapes are potatoes, beans, garlic, onions, kale, chard, tomatoes, cucumbers and zucchini.

Ideally your boulevard garden will look vibrant all year long. Edibles that hold up in the cold weather— blueberry bushes with their vibrant stem colour, beautiful kale, cabbage, cauliflower, Swiss chard, parsley, broad beans, corn salad and more—will give your garden four-season structure and make it appealing to walk by even in the dead of winter.

ADDITIONAL CONSIDERATIONS

MULCHING

This reduces evaporative water loss from the soil thus reducing water consumption. Avoid the use of "messy" or unsightly mulches such as straw and bark, which can blow or wash onto walkways and streets. Compost is one of the best mulches to use and has the added benefit of adding structure and nutrients to the soil.

USING COMPOST

Compost is the basis for good soil that in turn supports healthy plants. It also acts as a buffer for potential contaminants such as lead. In heavily trafficked areas this can be a concern. Scientists at Cornell University found that by adding large amounts (at least 25 percent by volume) of compost or well-rotted manure, and maintaining the soil's acid/alkaline balance near neutral (pH between 6.5 and 7.0), leaf and root crops (such as lettuce, spinach, potato and beet) were less likely to absorb lead. The more decomposed the organic matter, the more effective it became as a buffer.

ORGANIC FERTILIZERS AND PESTICIDES AND FUNGICIDES

Use organic fertilizers when you need to supplement your edibles' nutritional requirements. While mechanical controls are best, if you must use chemical controls for plant pests or diseases, look to using only organics. Despite your best efforts there is always the possibility of excess runoff from watering or overspray. These chemicals are very likely to wind up in storm drains.

PRUNING

In addition to the selection of appropriate trees and shrubs, regular monitoring and pruning of branches

Always check with city authorities before installing raised beds.

and foliage is required to ensure they do not protrude over sidewalks at head height or lower. For plants fronting onto streets or parking areas, trees should be trained and pruned to ensure lower branches will not come in contact with passing cars and trucks. As the trees grow, gardeners can prune off lower branches that could intrude over the footpath or road. This is best done while the trees are young so as to "lift" the canopy and encourage branching higher above the ground.

Tip: Avoid raised edges that are only a few centimetres above grade. Pedestrians may not be able to perceive that small a variation in grade and could trip. If allowable create an edge that is a minimum of 1ft. (30 cm) in height.

Shared gardens help to build security and
strong communities.

THE COMMUNITY GARDEN

Those lucky enough to have a sunny backyard or balcony can garden whenever they have the time and inclination. But for others, the answer is a community or allotment garden. And this is good news—community gardens beautify neighbourhoods and city blocks, bring people together and have even been proven to reduce crime as vacant lots are converted to dynamic food-producing spaces and idle hands become busy planting and plucking crops.

©Serge Lindsay

THIS GARDEN HAS BEEN CREATED AND CARED FOR IN PART BY

egp THE EDIBLE GARDEN PROJECT

www.ediblegardenproject.com

Food from this garden is donated to support people in need on the North Shore.

Fresh local fruits and vegetables contribute to healthy people, healthy communities, and a healthy planet.

For more information, or to get involved, contact:
THE EDIBLE GARDEN PROJECT
at the North Shore Neighbourhood House.
edible@vcn.bc.ca, 604-987-8138 x 209

The EGP is funded by Vancouver Coastal Health, North Shore in addition to the North Shore Neighbourhood House, and the City of North Vancouver

Use signage to educate the public as well as to provide contact information to those who might wish to join the garden community.

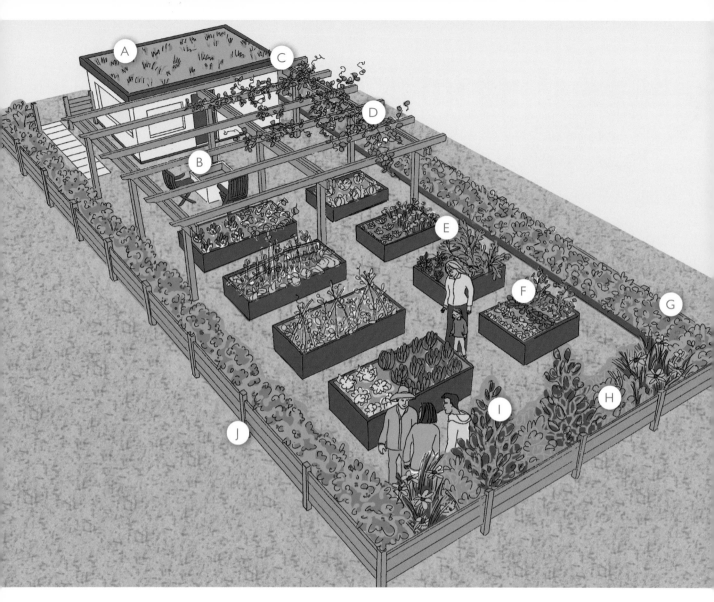

A   Adding a green roof to an outbuilding makes it extra environmentally friendly

B   A firepit or other focus creates a gathering area for the garden community

C   An outbuilding doubles as a potting shed and amenity facility for gardeners

D   Overhead structures support edible vines and can provide some shade

E   Planter beds are partitioned into squares 4 ft. (120 cm) by 4 ft. and assigned one plot per gardener—the square-foot garden principle allows for maximum efficiency

F   If accessible on all sides, beds are no more than 4 ft. (120 cm) wide to avoid the trampling of crops and soil

G   Perimeter fencing doubles as a framework for climbing edibles or espaliered trees

H   Perimeter planting is relegated to dwarf trees and fruit bushes, and doubles as a landscape barrier

I   Hard-surface pathways 3–4 ft. (90–120 cm) wide allow for comfortable walking and wheelbarrow access

J   Perimeter fencing defines public space from the private community garden

Community gardens beautify neighbourhoods and bring residents together.

THE PLAN

Lot Dimensions: 68 × 28 ft. (21 × 8.5 m)
Total Area of Edibles: 300 sq. ft. (28 sq. m)

DESIGNER NOTE

This community garden is designed as part of a condominium strata and located on top of a parkade. Beds are divided using the concept of the square foot garden (see page 119) for easy planting. The garden also serves as a place for meeting and entertaining, with a firepit and gathering area adjacent to a potting shed that doubles as a meeting room.

HOW DO YOU GET STARTED?

Community gardens are actually a derivative of the traditional row garden (see page 25), but on a much larger scale and with dozens of individual gardens. There are three scenarios for community gardens. Traditionally, tracts of land owned by local municipalities were turned into plots where gardeners could enter into a lease agreement for an individual plot. Also, private vacant lots were converted by gardeners who negotiated with owners for the use of their land.

More recently, community gardens are found within communally owned lands. As a landscape

Fill out edges with flowers that define the garden, attract pollinators and act as companion plants.

architect I have worked on many condominium and high-rise projects where allocated outdoor space within these developments is dedicated to growing food.

But what can you do if you don't have access to any of these options? How do you go about creating a community garden?

FIND YOUR GARDENERS FIRST!

Gather interested people—ideally, there should be at least 10 members keen to create and sustain a garden project. Survey the residents of your neighbourhood to see who is interested. Hold monthly meetings to develop and initiate plans, keep everyone posted on the garden's progress, and involve them in the process.

LOOK FOR LAND CANDIDATES

The next step is to check out your neighbourhood for a vacant lot that has the following conditions:

- Located within walking distance, or no more than a short drive from where you live.
- Receives six to eight hours of sun a day.
- Relatively flat (although slight slopes can be terraced) and free of large pieces of concrete left behind from demolition of structures. Any rubble or debris should be manageable—that is, removable

by volunteers without heavy equipment. It is possible to work with a site that is paved with concrete or asphalt by building raised beds or using containers that sit on the surface.

- Ideally, the land should be fenced with a gate wide enough for a vehicle to enter, or have the flexibility to allow a fence to be erected.
- Has access to water. If there has been water service to the site in the past, it is relatively inexpensive to get a new water meter installed (if one doesn't already exist). If the site has never been serviced by water, it may cost more for your water provider to install a lateral line from the street main to the lot and install a new meter. Depending on the size of your garden site, you will need a ½–1 in. water line.
- The soil should be workable or amendable. Have the site soil tested for fertility, pH and the presence of heavy metals. Land in industrial areas may be non-viable.

NEXT STEPS

Contact the landowner and ask for permission to use the property for a community garden. Establish a term for use of the site, and prepare and negotiate a lease—be sure to include a "hold harmless" waiver to protect the owner. Typically, groups lease garden sites from landowners for one dollar per year. You should attempt to negotiate a lease for at least three years.

Be prepared to purchase liability insurance to further protect the property owner (and yourself) should an accident occur at the garden.

FORM A GARDEN CLUB

Once your garden is up and running, create a club as an effective means of making decisions on communal issues such as design, development and maintenance. Functions typically handled by a garden club are establishing rules, planning events, reviewing applications, assigning plots, collecting dues, paying utilities and resolving conflicts.

DESIGN ELEMENTS

PLANTING BEDS

At least 15 plots should be available and assigned to community members. Without plots for individual participation, it is very difficult to achieve long-term community involvement.

Raised-bed plots, which are more expensive, should be no more than 4 ft. (1.2 m) wide to facilitate access to plants from all sides without stepping into the bed, and 8–12 ft. (2.5–3.6 m) long.

In-ground plots can be from 10 × 10 ft. (3 × 3 m) up to 20 × 20 ft. (6 × 6 m) square. Pathways between beds and plots should be at least 3–4 ft. (90–120 cm) wide to allow for wheelbarrows. The soil in both raised-bed and in-ground plots should be amended with aged compost or manure to improve fertility and increase organic-matter content.

IRRIGATION SYSTEM

A simple irrigation system with one hose bib or faucet for every four plots is most efficient. Hand watering with a hose is the most practical and affordable for individual plots (and almost a necessity when you start plants from seed). Drip and soaker-hose irrigation can be used in all areas of the garden for transplanted and established plants, especially deep-rooted fruit trees and ornamentals. If no one in your group is knowledgeable about irrigation, you might need some assistance in designing your system. Seek out a landscape contractor or garden-centre professional to help develop a basic layout and materials list.

Use raised beds filled with rich, well-drained soil for maximum harvests.

To ensure garden plots have easy access to water, locate hose bibs within 50 ft. (15 m).

Blueberries bring a unique combination of delicious fruit and striking ornamental beauty to the garden and landscape. I like to tuck them throughout the landscape as fillers and as a backdrop to ornamentals. They do double duty as foundation plantings or an informal hedge. The high levels of phytochemicals, thought to help protect against cancer and heart disease, mean blueberries are considered one of the top superfoods.

PERIMETER PLANTING

Perimeter landscaping outside the community garden can help to:

- Visually unify the garden from the outside. Plus, flowering plants can provide cut flowers.
- Act as attractants for pollinators that will in turn infiltrate into the edible garden. Contrastingly, herbs are well-suited to perimeter landscaping and can create barriers that deter unwanted pest insects that dislike the odour of their essential oils.
- Discourage unwanted visitors if plantings are thorny or armoured.

ORCHARDS AND EDIBLE SHRUBS

A small fruit-tree orchard, whose care and harvest can be shared by all the members, is a nice addition if the garden is permanent and large enough. The orchard can provide a buffer from the sun for people as well as for shade-loving plants.

Other permanent plantings such as blueberries, raspberries and currants can provide structure in the garden along with food.

SIGNAGE AND FENCING

Be sure to post a sign with the name of your garden, sponsors and a contact person's phone number for those wanting more information. If your community is bilingual, reflect that in all signage.

A perimeter fence preferably 6 ft. (2 m) tall with a drive-through gate is in my experience a key element of success. While you can't count on eliminating all acts of vandalism or theft, fencing will keep it to tolerably low levels. The higher the better, but if your objective is to be "neighbourly," consider augmenting the fence with thorny shrubs such as wild roses.

OUTBUILDINGS AND COMPOST AREA

A shed or other structure for storing tools, supplies and materials is important. Recycled metal shipping containers work very well and are pretty much vandal-proof.

Consider a shared composting area for the community garden.

ADDITIONAL CONSIDERATIONS

If you want to really go for it and have a permanent space for your community garden, here are some wonderful additions you can strive for:

- A children's area, which can include tiny garden plots, a sandbox and play equipment.
- A meeting area, which can range from a semi-circle of hay bales or tree stumps to a simple amphitheatre built of recycled broken concrete. Building a shade structure would be beneficial as well.
- A bench or picnic table where gardeners can relax and take a break—preferably in shade. If there are no shade trees on the site, a simple arbour can be

constructed from wood or pipe, and then planted with grapes, kiwis or other vines.

- A water fountain. This can be a simple drinking fountain attachment to a hose bib or faucet.
- A community bulletin board where rules, meeting notices and other important information is posted.
- Beehives are becoming popular additions but should be fenced off. The hives can be cabled and locked down to prevent vandals from knocking them over.

CHALLENGES

VANDALISM

In an urban situation it is inevitable that most gardens will experience occasional vandalism. The best action you can take is to replant immediately. Generally the vandals eventually become bored and stop. If you need more physical deterrents use thorny plants around fences.

SAFETY AND SECURITY

Invite the community officer from your local precinct to a garden meeting to share their suggestions on making the garden more secure. Ensure the garden is visible from the street—perimeter planting should on average be no higher than 3 ft. (90 cm) unless there is a high and secure fence around the garden.

MAINTENANCE

WEEDS

Gardeners usually visit their plots less during the winter time. Lower participation combined with rain tends to create a huge weed problem during the off-season. In addition to scheduled cleanup, crews can apply a thick layer of mulch or hay to the beds and paths to reduce weed proliferation and keep the garden looking nice.

Benches and seating areas bring gardeners together.

TRASH

It's important to get your compost system going right away and train gardeners how to use it. Without a compost strategy, large quantities of waste will build up, creating an eyesore that could hurt relationships with neighbours and the property owner. Waste can also become a fire and rodent hazard. Trash and recycling bins placed in accessible areas will help to keep the garden neat and tidy.

GARDENER DROP-OUT

While this is a management issue, it also affects the appearance of the garden. Anticipate that there can be a high rate of turnover in a community garden, with people signing up for plots and not following through. Be sure to have a clause in your agreement that states the gardener forfeits their right to the plot if they don't plant it within one month or don't maintain it.

Tip: For perimeter plantings exposed to pets and passersby, choose tough and drought-hardy picks that can take a beating and that you will not want to harvest.

Neatly trimmed boxwood hedges form the walls of
this traditional herb garden.

THE HERB GARDEN

Humans have had a long and loving relationship with herbs ever since they were first depicted in the Lascaux (France) cave paintings dating back to between 13,000 and 25,000 B.C. During the days of the ancient Greeks and Romans, herbs were used extensively as medicinal remedies. In medieval times herbs became aromatic foils, masking smells of the unwashed and the stink of rotting meat! This period was not favourable to the progress of herbs as medicine. In fact, the Catholic Church began burning herbalists, having associated them with both witchcraft and paganism.

Ironically, it fell to the medieval monks and religious leaders to grow vast herb gardens in their monasteries and carry the knowledge forward. These extensive displays became the basis for herb garden design as we know it today. Often enclosed or located within the confines of the cloister, these gardens consisted mostly of simple grid patterns of small square or rectangular beds. Pathways in between allowed for access to individual plots.

Knot gardens became a feature of English gardens in the mid-15th century when people had the time, money and security to make their gardens a haven for relaxation and fashion. Intellectual puzzles to amuse the spectator, knot gardens also had a practical and symbolic purpose in Tudor England, the knots representing the tying together of disparate elements—unity and strength.

Over time, herbs became more popular as flavourings for food, and the herb garden evolved to include fruits, vegetables and ornamental flowers. However, the basic bones or foundation of the traditional design have changed little.

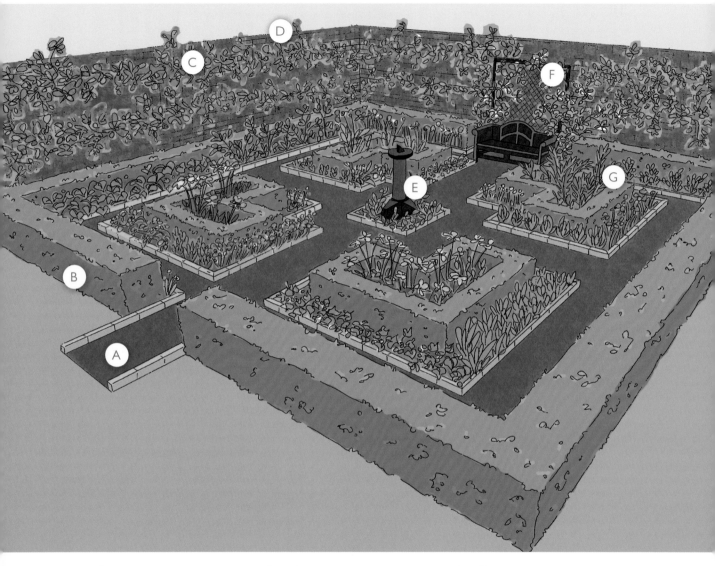

A   Oversized hard-surface pathways (a minimum of 4 ft./120 cm wide) add presence and ornamentation as well as functionality to the garden

B   Boxwood or other evergreen hedging creates permanent "bones" in the garden and adds a sense of formality

C   Espaliered fruit trees provide edibles as well as living sculpture on walls

D   Walls or fencing create a sense of enclosure and an outdoor room, and also provide microclimate systems that support more tender heat-loving edibles

E   A sundial, statuary or planter gives the garden a focal point

F   Ornamental benches can also act as focal points and provide opportunities for seating

G   Herbs planted inside hedging can be formally or randomly planted

THE PLAN

Lot Dimensions: 36 × 36 ft. (11 × 11 m)

DESIGNER NOTES

A traditional herb garden can easily be converted to fit a front or back outdoor space. The style is often formal with boxwood hedging that brings order to a diversity of herbs or edibles within its boundaries. Seating is integrated and a traditional sundial provides a focal point. Alternatively, you could replace the dial with a fountain or beautiful oversized pot of topiary.

This herb garden was designed for a small backyard or as part of a larger space in the formal style. Hedges and walls create a sense of an enclosure or outdoor room.

DESIGN ELEMENTS

SITE SELECTION

Herb gardens are a little more unique than most edible gardens in that site selection and soils become very important. Most of the popular herbs you will want to grow prefer the hot, dry Mediterranean climate and well-drained or even slightly gravelly soils. These plants require at least six to eight hours of direct sunlight a day to produce the oils that account for their aromatic flavours. Similarly, most herbs do not require highly fertile ground. Good soil will produce excessive foliage and less flavour. And few of the key herbs grow in wet soils, so excellent drainage is a must. There is a smattering of herbs, however—such as mint, angelica and lovage—that do thrive in fairly moist soil, so group these moisture lovers in a damp spot.

If the herb garden is primarily culinary in nature, select a site close to your kitchen—you will be much more likely to harvest them daily if you don't have to trek down the length of the yard to collect them.

Herb gardens can contain fruits as well as vegetables—use your imagination!

©Sergei Lindsay

WHAT'S YOUR STYLE? FORMAL VERSUS INFORMAL

A formal herb garden is shaped in a geometrical pattern and usually more ornamental than an informal variation. The geometric shapes are often divided and then subdivided into smaller sections, usually by paths or dwarf hedges. Large blocks of the same plant are often used to reinforce these principles. Knot gardens are a step up in ornamentation with a series of interweaving miniature hedges that create intricate patterns.

The informal garden doesn't have a specific pattern to it and the beds contain mixtures of herbs, fruits and vegetables. Walkways wind through beds, much like a common garden and can be as simple as gravel or stepping stones.

BED LAYOUT

FORMAL GARDENS

Formal bed layouts can use the geometry of circles, squares, rectangles and even triangles. The keys are consistency and repetition of the same elements and keeping your overall pattern very symmetrical. A high-use utilitarian herb garden can be simple rows of beds no more than 4 ft. (120 cm) wide if accessed from two sides, or 3 ft. (90 cm) if accessed from just one side.

A winding gravel pathway edged with stones adds an informal element to a more structured garden.

Mixed beds, on the other hand, are designed for function as well as beauty and have a little more flexibility in their layout. Often-harvested herbs such as parsley can line the perimeter, reducing compaction of soil and damage to adjacent plants from the foot traffic of harvesters. Stepping stones or tiny gravel strips can also be used to reduce damaging effects. These same herbs can also be designed in as part of the pattern thus reinforcing the geometry and adding ornamentation.

KNOT GARDENS

A knot garden provides contrasting foliage colours, with divisions that provide neat pockets for growing individual herbs. Essentially a tapestry or piece of living art, its patterns should be filled in with a limited plant palette for maximum effect. Ideally, the edibles grown will not overwhelm the diminutive nature of the knot garden. Possible patterns for a modern knot garden include brick circle, brick diamond, square within a square, diagonal paths, interlocking diamonds, oblongs and right angles, diamonds and squares, diamonds in rectangles, and wheel beds.

For inspiration, look at knot patterns in herb books or references on ancient cultures or even history books. Keep in mind that the more complicated the pattern, the more time-consuming the maintenance will be to keep hedges perfectly clipped and hard edges retained. But on the upside, these gardens provide year-round interest.

For herb gardens typical of an urban yard—less than 20 × 20 ft. (6 × 6 m)—sections are filled with small- or medium-sized plants complementary to the overall design. Taller herbs will spoil the design once fully grown. Each individual section of the design should be planted with one variety of herbs to give a block of bold colour.

A less labour-intensive approach is to give your herb garden the bones of a formal layout with symmetrical beds and paths and then fill it in with exuberant herb plants that can be allowed to mature, fill in and spread without constant supervision.

At the very least, allow 6 ft. (2 m) square for a knot garden—anything smaller will not allow for weaving of lines.

WALKWAYS

The paths should be at least 2 ft. (60 cm) wide for basic access to plants and wider, 4 ft. (120 cm) or more, if the walks and gardens are making a design statement such as an entry sequence to the front door.

Walkway material should always be functional as well as appropriate for your design. Brick, stone pavers or fine gravel retained by an edge lend themselves to ornamental formal design. Lawn, mulch, stepping stones and loose gravel are more appropriate for informal or utilitarian gardens.

Tip: Two intersecting paths dividing a square garden into four equal parts is a pleasing, simple and well-tested pattern.

Materials used for edging can include wood, stone, and bricks standing up on end.

©Serga Lindsay

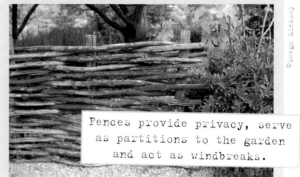

Fences provide privacy, serve as partitions to the garden and act as windbreaks.

©Serga Lindsay

FOCAL PIECES

The centre of a formal herb garden is usually the focal point and a place to make a personal statement. This can take the form of a garden ornament such as a bird bath, a planter, a feature plant or topiary, or the often-used sundial. It can also be an opportunity to provide seating framed within an arbour.

EDGINGS

Hedging using boxwood or lavender is the traditional way to define edges around your herb beds. Wattle fences were also popular and these are created by weaving green spring saplings in between upright posts. Other materials to use could be raised wood planters or bricks on end. For a modern twist consider using metal edgings or contemporary materials like architectural concrete.

PLANTINGS

In the culinary world most herbs used in cooking come from dry, hot climates. These plants often exhibit small, beautifully textured leaves, many greyish in colour or even hairy with flowers small and far between—all of which prevent excess moisture loss and sun damage. It is not by coincidence that many plants used have a similar feel typical of the herb-garden style. Also, many of the popular herbs are perennials or woody shrubs, which come back every year.

It is important to focus on texture and foliage colour to unify these gardens. Also consider scale and the complexity of your planting design. For small urban gardens, less is more and small- to medium-sized plants with smaller leaves and textures will complement and reinforce a structured formal garden. Whereas, taller, showier plants will add more interest and dimension to larger or informal herb gardens.

For formal or knot gardens I recommend using dwarf boxwood (*Buxus sempervirens* 'Suffruticosa'), as it is a true miniature hedging plant. To lighten up your space or add contrast use the slow-growing variegated boxwood (*Buxus sempervirens* 'Variegata') or germander (*Teucrium chamaedrys*).

Other edging plants to consider, for those not interested in clipping perfect boxes, are dwarf lavenders such as *Lavandula angustifolia* 'Nana' or *Lavandula angustifolia* 'Thumbelina Leigh,' which will not get woody and out of shape over time. For a milder climate (zone 7 or warmer), boxwood hebe (*Hebe buxifolia* 'Nana') will maintain a tidy semi-rounded shape.

BOUNDARIES AND FENCING

Almost all herb gardens benefit from some sort of defining border. The most permanent boundary for the herb garden is a wall. However this does not come without expense. Fences are less expensive and faster to build than walls and they can also provide privacy, serve as partitions and act as windbreaks.

SITTING AREAS

Historically herb gardens were devoted to cultivation of plants. Access paths were a common feature and it was not until medieval times that seating areas became popular. Prefabricated wood or stone benches can be framed within an arbour or trellis of scented flowers or herbs to become strong focal points.

A bench of turf or creeping herbs and flowers was a common feature in medieval gardens. Built like a broad double wall, these seats can be filled with aromatic plants such as chamomile. There should be two large flat stones set amongst the plants for sitting on during damp weather.

Tip: Be sure to plant your most aromatic plants such as thyme and lavender next to seating areas. Shade-tolerant mints can be planted under a bench to provide a soothing scent every time you brush them with your feet.

DESIGNER TIPS

A less labour-intensive approach is to give your herb garden the bones of a formal layout with symmetrical beds and paths and then fill it with exuberant herbs such as borage, anise hyssop and bee balm, which can be allowed to mature and spread without constant attention.

Borage is the magic bullet of companion planting, helping almost everything—from strawberries to cucurbits (cucumbers, gourds) and tomatoes—by attracting predatory insects and repelling detrimental ones. It is a magnet for bees, and the flowers and young leaves can be used in salads.

To add interest to a small garden, consider colourful foliage. Basil is available in rich purples in addition to shades of green; sage comes in purple as well as variegated yellow and green; thyme is offered in a rainbow of hues.

Place low creepers like thyme and chamomile on opposite path edges to complement each other.

Contain more aggressive herbs like mint and lemon balm in pots to discourage them from spreading aggressively throughout your garden.

With thoughtful design, everyone can experience
the benefits that come from spending time
in the garden.

THE ENABLING GARDEN

An enabling garden or barrier-free garden is designed for those—young and old—with physical, mental or sensory impairments. In many cases, all it takes is a little tweaking to remove a few flaws that are inhibiting someone from enjoying the experience of an edible garden.

Unused walls and fences are perfect planting opportunities for those with limited reach.

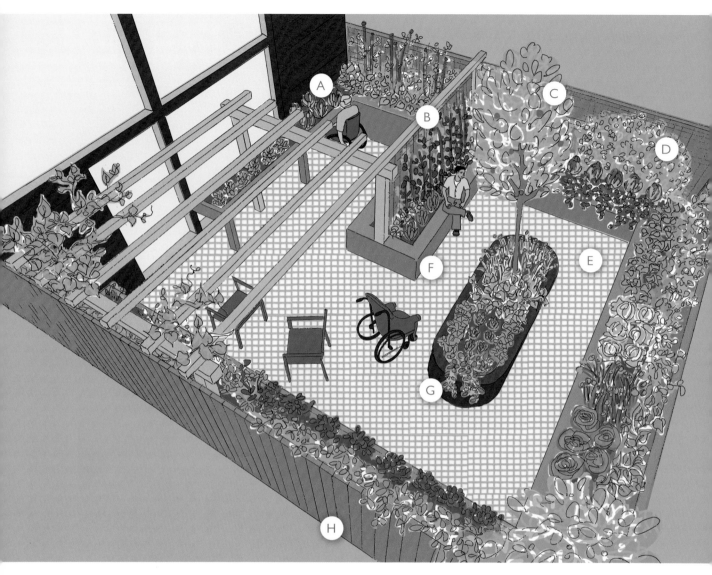

A   Raised planters on legs allow for easy wheelchair access

B   Arbours support edible vines and provide shade opportunities

C   Dwarf fruit trees provide shade and allow for easy reaching

D   Wall-mounted trellises and planters enable edibles to grow vertically

E   Hard and even surfaces with nominal cross slopes allow for safe walking and wheelchair access—a minimum width of 4 ft. (120 cm) width is required for pathways, along with generous turning radiuses

F   Planter walls are widened to provide opportunities for seating

G   Raised beds a minimum height of 18 in. (45 cm) provide comfortable seating and easy-reach gardens

H   Perimeter fencing provides enclosure and doubles as a framework for climbing edibles or espaliered trees

Planter beds on legs allow a gardener in a wheelchair to pull right up.

COMMON CHALLENGES TO CONSIDER

MOBILITY AND REACH

Something as simple as a gravel path may become an impediment for someone restricted to a wheelchair or required to use a walking stick. And mobility challenges with bending and reaching, compromised balance or coordination, or even a shuffling gait, can make the smallest obstacles overwhelming.

VISUAL IMPAIRMENT

Vision can become limited in various ways—from a reduction in depth perception to sensitivity to the glare of shiny or reflective surfaces. Our eyes may start to filter out darker colours where we see yellows, reds and oranges more easily than dark blues or greens.

SENSITIVITY TO WEATHER EXTREMES

Elderly people can become highly sensitive to extremes of weather and rapid changes in temperature.

MINOR IMPAIRMENT OF MENTAL FACULTIES

Memory loss or slowness in reaction to hazards can put some people at risk. In some cases, judgment may also be impaired, which can be of particular concern in an edible garden.

EROSION OF CONFIDENCE

Lack of self assurance is the prime reason elderly people in particular lose connection with their outdoor environment. As we age, we often feel increasingly more vulnerable about getting around or tackling tasks that we once leapt into without hesitation.

A Raised beds a minimum height of 18 in. (45 cm) provide comfortable seating and easy-reach gardens

B Dwarf fruit trees provide shade and allow for easy reaching

C Wall-mounted trellises and planters enable edibles to grow vertically

D Perimeter fencing provides enclosure and doubles as a framework for climbing edibles or espaliered trees

E Arbours support edible vines and provide shade opportunities

F Raised planters on legs allow for easy wheelchair access

G Planter walls are widened to provide opportunities for seating

H Hard and even surfaces with nominal cross slopes allow for safe walking and wheelchair access—a minimum width of 4 ft. (120 cm) width is required for pathways, along with generous turning radiuses

Pergolas can provide a frame for climbers, with shady seating below.

Bold colours and leaf patterns help those with poor vision to differentiate between edibles.

THE PLAN

Lot Dimensions: 25 × 25 ft. (7.5 × 7.5 m)

Total Area for Edibles: 287 sq. ft. (26.6 sq. m) in planters, 283 sq. ft. (26 sq. m) vertically

DESIGNER NOTE

This design is based on a narrow lot configuration of just 28 ft. (8.5 m) wide.

DESIGN ELEMENTS

KEEP IT SAFE AND SIMPLE

The garden should be safe, comfortable and uncomplicated. Therefore, the layout should be simple, avoiding curves and intricate patterns. Landmarks or reference points can be used to assist orientation. Ornaments and seating are best recessed from pathways so not to become tripping hazards. Consider a secure fence and gate a minimum of 6 ft. (2 m) high around the garden to prevent mentally disoriented individuals from wandering.

PATHWAYS

Pathways a minimum of 4 ft (1.2 m) wide allow access for wheelchairs and for people to walk side by

side. If a wheelchair will be used, remember to allow enough space for manoeuvring—a manual chair has a turning circle of 5 ft. (1.5 m); a powered version needs 6 ft. (1.8 m). Changes in level are a common hazard in gardens, so add ramps and avoid steps wherever possible. Ensure slopes do not exceed a grade of 5 percent and that their cross slopes do not surpass 2 percent.

Path materials should be firm and well-draining, non-slip, non-reflective and have good traction. Tailor the surface to the gardener. For example, decomposed granite is suitable for people in wheelchairs but not for those on crutches. Concrete is an all-round appropriate choice if it is tinted to reduce glare and jointing is not so deep it creates a tripping hazard. Newer rubberized paving materials are firm enough for wheelchairs and will cushion falls. Concrete pavers can also work well as long as they are installed properly—any shifting may cause tripping hazards.

If possible create a change in texture along the edge of a path to help people with visual impairments recognize by touch that they are in danger of stepping off it. Also, use materials with strong, contrasting colours to help overcome the visual confusion of moving from an area of light to shade. Finally, avoid raised edges, another tripping risk.

GARDEN BEDS

Garden beds or raised planters will be more manageable if the gardener can reach across them easily. Make beds no wider than 2 ft. (60 cm) if you have access from only one side, or 4 ft. (120 cm) wide if you can reach from all sides.

A raised bed is ideal for wheelchair users and those with limited mobility, with the edges of the garden working as convenient seating. Heights can range from 18–30 in. (45–75 cm) with 2 ft. (60 cm) optimal for both seated and standing gardeners. Planter boxes on legs allow for someone in a wheelchair to pull right up.

GO VERTICAL

Another way to increase the amount of accessible planting space is to consider unused walls, fences and overhangs. A trellis or netting attached to a vertical surface with planters at the base creates a support for climbing plants. Enhanced with shelves, brackets and hangers, unused walls, fences, decks and balcony railings become platforms for any number of window boxes, smaller pots, baskets and decorative containers—all within easy reach.

SEATING AND SHELTER

Use roof overhangs, arbours or pergolas to protect from the elements. Pergolas or arbours can provide a frame for climbers with shaded seating below. A specimen tree can act like a shady umbrella to give respite from the sun.

Use roof overhangs to advantage. Benches in dark colours absorb the sun's heat so that seating dries faster. Sturdy seating with backs and arms should be provided for those who need support when sitting for long periods of time.

LANDMARKS

For larger gardens, landmarks or reference points should be used to assist with orientation. A bird bath or fountain is a good focal point. A key specimen or mass planting can create emphasis within the space and also help a gardener remain clear on where they are situated within the garden.

PLANTS

If you would like to grow fruit trees, select espaliered or cordon-trained varieties—these grow at a lower level and are easy to reach.

Choose plants that are simple to maintain (requiring less fertilizing and little pruning, and disease and pest resistant). Plantings should not sprawl over pathways and must be thornless and non-toxic. Avoid poisonous bulbs too, like daffodils, which could be mistaken for an onion by an impaired gardener.

For the visually challenged, strong contrasts in flower and foliage colours will add greatly to the gardener's ability to see and savour their plantings. A mix of leaf, flower and vegetable shapes also helps them to define one plant from the next, while fragrance will also add to their experience—try a selection of aromatic herbs or a tantalizing clump of familiar-smelling tomato bushes. At the same time you may want to avoid plants that attract large numbers of bees or other insects that may pose a threat to a vulnerable gardener.

THE BALCONY GARDEN

No yard? No problem. Apartment dwellers needn't miss out on the pleasure of growing their own fruits and veggies. If you can grow it on the ground you can use these simple techniques to grow it on a balcony without compromising your living space or style. The key is to make every inch of your space count, including floors, walls, ceilings and even railings.

©iStockphoto.com/sdorell

A Permanent larger pots are integrated to support larger edibles such as tomatoes and peppers

B Trellises on walls support edible vines

C Overhead structure supports edible vines and creates a sense of enclosure

D Edible plants are located according to their light requirements, with shade-tolerant plants located at the back of the patio space

E The patio furniture should reflect the interior decor

F Moveable pots of edibles match the style of pots inside the residence, providing continuity

G The balcony's flooring material matches flooring in the adjacent interior spaces

THE PLAN

Balcony Dimensions: 10 × 7 ft. (3 × 2 m)

Total Area for Edibles: 50 sq. ft. (4.6 sq. m) (vertically and horizontally) plus 10 sq. ft. (1 sq. m) in planter.

Total: 60 sq. ft. (5.6 sq. m)

DESIGNER NOTES

This small city balcony is a mere 70 sq. ft. (6.5 sq. m) yet still provides enough edibles to keep a single person going with their favourite vegetables. One wall has been allocated for a generous (30 × 48 × 30 in. or 75 × 120 × 75 cm) drip-irrigated container that can support a permanent fruit-bearing grape or kiwi vine in a back corner. This can be trained as an overhead green roof. Annual vine crops such as tomatoes, cucumbers and squash can be planted along the back edge of the planter and allowed to grow up a trellis fixed to the wall. The front of the container is planted with colourful salad and quick-growing crops ('Neon Lights' Swiss chard) or trailing edibles such as 'Tumbling Tom' tomatoes and strawberries that produce runners. Smaller pots can also be tucked into patio containers for ornamentation as well as harvesting.

If light is a problem, stick with cool-season crops that don't mind less sun, and consider using grow lights to supplement lighting requirements.

DESIGN ELEMENTS

BEFORE YOU BEGIN

RULES AND REGULATIONS

Before starting your balcony garden, check with building management for legal and safety issues and confirm that the changes you wish to make are allowable. Also, be aware of city bylaws pertaining to what you can place beside or on top of balcony railings.

Think of your balcony as a valuable visual extension of the living area it adjoins. Complement the style of your interior by using similar materials and colours on your patio.

YOUR DECK SPECS

Strata management can supply you with other vital information such as the maximum weight your balcony can withstand. While most are designed to bear the load of a standard table with chairs and a few pots, larger containers (the equivalent of half a wine barrel) loaded with wet soil can weigh 200 lb. (90 kg) or more. Lightweight alternatives to traditional pots and soil will most likely be required.

Drainage is another consideration. Ideally your balcony would have an integrated drainage system, otherwise excess water may drip onto your neighbour below. Alternatively, using plant saucers or rubber mats can help mitigate this problem (although you should empty the saucers so that your plants are not sitting in water).

DO AN INVENTORY

Understanding your patio's exposure to sun and wind will help you choose the right plant for the right place. Full sun means more than six hours of sunlight per day; this is required by all warm-season plants such as

A balcony garden can easily keep a single person supplied with fresh vegetables.

peppers and tomatoes. Partial shade or between four to six hours of sun is acceptable for cool-season crops such as lettuce. Constant winds at high altitudes can dry out containers very quickly or knock them over. If this is your situation, select tough and resilient edible plants and larger containers to provide a windbreak. Also take note of views you may want to screen— this is where a tall plant can provide you with the canopy you need.

THE CREATIVE PART

The same design principles apply on a balcony as on the ground. However, one of the advantages of a balcony garden is that if you don't get things exactly right the first year you can move elements around the next.

CONNECT INSIDE WITH OUT

Think of your balcony as a visual extension of the living area it adjoins. Complement the style of your interior by using similar materials and colours. For example, using the same flooring inside and out is one of the simplest and most effective ways to integrate the balcony with the indoors. Use the same style of furniture you have on the inside or perhaps you can move a few pieces outside. Also continue your interior colour scheme outside by painting adjoining outdoor walls. Standing a few pots (of similar style) on the interior floor as well as on the balcony will strengthen the visual link between the two areas.

EVERY INCH COUNTS

Use floors, walls and ceilings to grow your edibles. Shelves, hooks, brackets and wall-mounted urns are great balcony space-savers. Walls can be used to support trellises and vine plants such cucumbers, beans and indeterminate tomatoes. Living-wall systems can also be mounted where space permits.

Make use of existing beams or build a faux arbour into the ceiling to support vigorous and permanent vines such as grapes. Alternatively, hooks supported by a stud in the ceiling work well for hanging baskets and (bylaws allowing) railings make great supports for bracket-mounted planter boxes.

CONTAINERS FOR PLANTING

Use containers that work with the style of your interior decor. The larger the container the less watering you will have to do and the bigger the crops you can grow. Choose lightweight materials such as plastic, wood or fibreglass and powder-coated aluminum, all of which can overwinter outdoors to save you storage space. And don't forget that smaller containers bursting with edibles serve beautifully as centrepieces for your patio table.

Tip: Grow mint around your patio to repel ants, along with basil to discourage flies and mosquitoes.

FURNITURE

A dining table or some form of seating is a must for entertaining but should be small enough to leave room for people to manoeuvre. Café-sized tables work best for small spaces and bench seats that have built-in storage are convenient for hiding tools or coiling hoses.

PLANTING

RIGHT PLANT, RIGHT PLACE

With a little creativity you can find an edible for just about any growing condition. Cluster edibles with similar maintenance requirements for striking arrangements. Look to cool-season crops if you are planting in shade or celebrate your sun with Mediterranean herbs (rosemary, thyme, etc.) or tomatoes.

PLANT COMPOSITION

Use different container and plant sizes to create visual interest. Mix edible flowering plants such as nasturtiums with your vegetables to add a colourful punch. Repeat plant types and colours so your patio garden does not look spotty with one of this and one of that. And play complementary colours off each other.

THINK SMALL

Almost every edible you can think of nowadays comes in miniature or patio versions suited to a smaller space. Look to cultivars with high yields and minimal space requirements.

SOIL

Use lightweight soil with high water-holding capacity to minimize the load on your balcony. To reduce the soil weight in large containers, fill the bottom third with crushed plastic cell packs or Styrofoam peanuts. A layer of landscape cloth will keep the soil from washing through.

My favourite centrepiece is a 'Meyer' lemon in a vibrant red container. Barely 2 ft. (60 cm) in diameter, this plant provides loads of lemons all winter—and the fragrance of the flowers is fabulous!

ADDITIONAL CONSIDERATIONS

ACCESS

Balcony gardening usually means bringing the bags of soil, containers and plants up several floors. Be sure all the fixtures you choose will fit into the elevator.

WATERING

If you are lucky enough to have a tap on your patio, you can hook up a drip-irrigation system with an automatic timer so that you won't have to remember when to water. Alternatively, try connecting a lightweight coil hose to your kitchen or bathroom tap.

STORAGE

Plan to store tools, bags of soil, extra containers, fertilizer, cushions and anything that cannot overwinter outdoors.

With a little planning you can have the ultimate
edible outdoor room.

THE URBAN COURTYARD GARDEN

The two variations of this design are based on the ever-increasing popularity of townhouse gardens. Typically these spaces are less than 20 × 20 ft. (6 × 6 m) and attached to row or townhouse units of similar widths.

©Judywhite/GardenPhotos.com

Many townhomes have front entrances that also serve as living areas.

A   A cool colour palette gives the illusion of more space in the garden

B   Fruit trees work as focal points and also act as an overhead canopy for the seating area

C   Walls create the sense of an outdoor room and provide an opportunity for trellising to support climbing edibles

D   Patio furniture reflects the style of the interior decor

E   Repeated elements such as planters create unity and the illusion of more space in the garden

F   The courtyard's flooring material matches flooring in the adjacent interior spaces

A living wall is a gorgeous and functional privacy screen for townhome gardens.

PLAN A

Lot Dimensions: 28 × 12.5 ft. (8.5 × 3.8 m)

Total Area for Edibles: 27 sq. ft. (2.5 sq. m) in planters and 100 sq. ft. (9.3 sq. m) vertically

DESIGNER NOTE

This contemporary urban courtyard focuses on a main dining table where an apple tree selected for brilliant-red fruit provides an overhead canopy. Black-cube pots planted in each corner overflow with red peppers and trailing strawberries, complementing the minimalist colour scheme of white, red and yellow. Bay-tree topiaries planted in each pot provide year-round interest and a sculptural element to the garden. Metal latticework inset into architectural concrete walls supports cucumbers that provide punctuation points of yellow flowers in addition to green fruit. Pennsylvania bluestone forms the flooring and matches the grey and black tones of the courtyard's hard elements (dining table and chairs, concrete walls and planter pots).

PLAN B

Lot Dimensions: 15 × 20 ft. (4.5 × 6 m)

Total Area of Edibles: 145 sq. ft. (13.5 sq. m) in planters and 200 sq. ft. (18.6 sq. m) vertically, plus one fruit tree

DESIGNER NOTE

This courtyard is the ultimate when it comes to maximizing a small area. Every bit of space possible is used for growing edibles. The courtyard has places for barbecuing and dining. It even has a small firepit for after-dinner relaxation.

DESIGN ELEMENTS

Unless you are opting for the "jungle look," the key ingredients to consider in creating a useable, chic outdoor space are style, materials, finishes and colour—all should be in tune with each other and with the architecture of the adjoining house.

Many townhomes have front entrances that also serve as living areas. Think beyond the traditional lawn and shrubs to create curb appeal using edibles. Vertical elements such as lattices covered in edible vines, trees or fruit-producing shrubs like currants can create a sense of enclosure and privacy from the street. Thorn-armoured shrubs like raspberries can serve as a hedge to discourage intruders.

THINK LIKE AN INTERIOR DESIGNER

Use the same principles you would use for interior design. Keep it bold and simple. Like a balcony garden (see page 99), connect the inside with the outside.

A Repeated elements such as planters create unity and the illusion of more space in the garden

B Benches are integrated or planters widened to multi-task as seating opportunities

C Spaces are divided to add additional functions such as this firepit area

D Fruit trees work as focal points and also act as an overhead canopy for the seating area or as dividers in the garden

E Space-saving edibles such as columnar fruit trees add dimension as well as edibles to the garden

F Walls create the sense of an outdoor room and provide an opportunity for trellising to support climbing edibles

G A cool colour palette gives the illusion of more space in the garden

H Patio furniture reflects the style of the interior decor

I Planters are widened to multi-task as seating opportunities

J The courtyard's flooring material matches flooring in the adjacent interior spaces

Use walls and overhead structures to create opportunities to grow food. Latticework can support a variety of vine vegetables that double as screens to add privacy and enclose your space.

Lavender is my absolute favourite garden perennial. In an informal flowerbed the blooming plants provide a cloud of hazy colour from white, pink or pale purple through to intense blues or violets. When not flowering, mature lavenders form dense and neat mounds of foliage, ranging from grey to green, and are perfect as low hedging or pathway edging.

PROVIDE A SENSE OF ENCLOSURE & PRIVACY

Living in close quarters means a gardener may want her courtyard to screen the view into it (rather than out of it). A sense of enclosure created by "walls" will not only shield you from the "uglies" beyond your space but will also give you a sense of privacy. Walls are usually more visual than literal—a free-standing vine-covered trellis or hedge does a good job of screening a small space (perhaps less than 10 sq. ft./.9 sq. m) without making it feel claustrophobic.

Plant an open roof or arbour with vines to create a cozy space that remains bright and welcoming. A retractable awning is a flexible way to give a sense of enclosure and the ability to cover the courtyard in winter extends the time you can use it.

SCALE IT UP OR DOWN

An aspect of design you do have control over is scale. A grouping of tables and chairs that feels comfortable in an open patio area may seem cramped in a walled courtyard. Look for alternatives like café tables and chairs that work well in a small space. Scale also comes into play when selecting plants. In terms of both design and horticulture, it works better to have fewer, larger containers than a multitude of tiny pots.

OPTICAL ILLUSIONS

Make spaces appear bigger by strategically placing mirrors in the garden to create the illusion of more light and area. Use colour to your advantage: cool tones like blue and green tend to make objects recede, while hot hues like purple and red give the illusion of things being closer.

MULTI-TASKING

Planter beds can also function as bench seats adjacent to a table. Simply widen the edge to allow for a comfortable seat width. Free-standing benches can do double duty by providing storage for tools and materials.

REPEAT, REPEAT

To create a feel of unity and harmony, repeat common elements such as planter pots. One-offs give a sense of clutter and make your space seem smaller.

ADD PERMANENT SCULPTURAL ELEMENTS

Look to using edibles as organic sculptural pieces. Chose those with year-round impact: think evergreen shrubs, trees and herbs. Bay topiaries in pots, for example, are evergreen elements in the garden that provide "bones" and look great all year round. Similarly, clipped lavender and rosemary in repeating pots give a stylish rhythm and unity to a formal garden.

GO VERTICAL TO MAXIMIZE SPACE

Use walls and overhead structures to create opportunities to grow food. Latticework can support a variety of vine vegetables that double as screens for privacy and enclosure. Walls or arbours can anchor hanging planters filled with trailing edibles such as cucumbers or upside-down tomatoes. Arbours also provide a permanent support for fruit-bearing vines.

UNIFY AND REPEAT

To create a sense of unity, use groupings of containers with similar plants of complementary textures and colours. Stick to a specific colour palette as well. For example, if you are trying to create a contemplative herb garden primarily composed of greens and muted colours, do not mix your muted palette with a blast of riotous red-hot nasturtiums.

CHOOSE MULTI-TASKING PLANTS

Think outside the box and look at edibles to perform a variety of functions in the garden. For example, thyme is not only an excellent edging plant but can be used between stepping stones. Vine plants work for screening on trellises and as trailers in raised planters. Grapevines and fruit trees double as shade plants for outdoor rooms during hot summer months. Thorny fruit-bearing shrubs are good barriers on the fence line to deter pests or intruders.

Similarly, espaliered fruit—where trees or shrubs are trained to grow in a flat plane against a wall, often in a symmetrical pattern—doubles as organic art. Because it hugs the wall, it doesn't encroach on space the way a hedge or free-standing tree can. A free-standing espaliered planting also provides another dimension and sense of depth within the garden. You can purchase espaliered trees ready-made from your local nursery; all you need do is keep them pruned to retain their shape.

GROW SMALL BIG PLANTS

Growing miniature fruit trees doesn't mean miniature fruit! The fruit tree is usually grafted onto a dwarf rootstock resulting in a small-sized plant that produces normal-sized fruit. Miniatures are great for pots, low hedges and courtyards. If space is really limited try multi-grafted fruit trees with two or three varieties grafted onto one rootstock. This also allows cross pollination, again, saving on space. If you have a narrow bed alongside a wall or fence, try a 'Ballerina' pillar apple tree. Its tall upright growth is reminiscent of a pole and when it fruits, it is laden with tons of apples.

Tip: Use self-fertile fruit trees where no cross pollination is required are great for the smaller garden.

THE GOURMET GARDEN KITCHEN

Not so long ago, outdoor cooking meant a tiny backyard grill and harried trips to and from the kitchen, with dinner served on a wobbly plastic table.

Today, people increasingly see gardens as extensions of their indoor spaces. Manufacturers have responded by providing an array of outdoor kitchen appliances ranging from the simple barbecue to large-capacity grills. And for the gourmet there are sinks, cabinetry and wine fridges for the ultimate in convenience and climate control. Outdoor furniture has also taken a giant leap from the rickety picnic table to high-end dining- and living-room sets. Combine all this with an edible landscape and you have the makings of the ultimate gourmet garden.

©Arcila Designs

A Trellising provides enclosure and supports climbing edible vines

B Kitchen facilities include a barbecue, fridge, sink and storage space

C Permanent soil-filled "living walls" host a wide variety of edible plantings

D A canopy frames the space and supports edible vines and overhead comfort systems such as heaters

E Counter space integrates planters for edibles

F Seating for relaxing and dining is integrated in the kitchen facility

G Durable impermeable flooring allows for easy cleanup and resistance to stains

THE PLAN

Kitchen and Planter Dimensions: 16 × 15.5
   ft. (4.8 × 4.7 m)
Total Area of Edibles: Planters: 38 sq. ft. (3.6 sq. m);
   Edible Walls and Ceilings: 200 sq. ft. (18.6 sq. m)

DESIGNER NOTE

This is the ultimate design for those foodies who want to grow, cook and eat out of their own outdoor kitchen. This kitchen design boasts a barbecue, fridge, sink and ample storage (wine fridge, anyone?) under the counters. Fresh produce can be picked and prepared literally minutes before eating.

DESIGN ELEMENTS

LOCATION, LOCATION, LOCATION

The first decision is where to position your outdoor gourmet kitchen—against the house or further afield in the yard?

Setting up closer to the house may enable you to take advantage of existing overhead protection or an opportunity to add inexpensive awnings. Installation of electrical, gas and water lines will be easier and less expensive the closer you are. And there definitely is a convenience factor if food prep is to take place in the indoor kitchen.

On the downside, though, grills and cooking appliances close to the house may pose a fire hazard; in addition, cooking smells and smoke may drift indoors. And although probably a little less convenient, kitchens and eating areas located away from the house and well into the garden can become an enchanting retreat.

PLANNING YOUR SPACE

The next step is to envision how you want to cook, entertain and live in your outdoor space. Begin by considering how many people you typically entertain, at what times of day and in what seasons. This will help to define whether you may want an enclosure such as an overhead canopy or comfort systems such as heaters. Also, think about what kind of entertaining you like to do—is it mainly casual or more formal dining? This will define what type of furniture you may need and how it will integrate with your kitchen functions. In terms of cooking amenities, are you happy with a simple grill or do you need it all, including the kitchen sink?

Finally, as a good portion of your garden space will be allocated to hard structures, it is important to think of overall style. Do you want to complement your existing house and garden or do you want to make a statement? Before you begin, start with a checklist of questions both general and specific regarding your outdoor kitchen. Ask yourself:

- How self-sufficient do you want the outdoor kitchen to be?
- How will it interface with your indoor kitchen when cooking or entertaining?
- What will be the pattern of traffic between your indoor and outdoor kitchen?
- How often do you grill?
- How many people do you wish to be able to entertain at one time?
- Will you need to be able to accommodate a bartender and/or caterer?
- What is your equipment wish list? Kitchen accessories and appliances?
- Do you want the counter built at one height or with split levels so guests can sit at the bar counter?
- And how many people do you want your counter to accommodate?

Built-in counters with stools can provide attractive eating areas if you do not have the space or inclination for a formal outdoor dining table.

APPLIANCES AND COUNTER SPACE

An outdoor kitchen layout follows the same work-triangle principle as an indoor version. The space connecting the stove, sink and refrigerator should be between 4–8 ft. (1.2–2.4 m) long.

Once you have a list of the equipment you want to include and dimensions, you can calculate how much counter space is required. A good rule of thumb is 16 in. (40 cm) of space between each accessory, based on the size of a serving platter. Countertops are generally 36–38 in. (90–96 cm) high. Bar counter heights vary from 42–46 in. (105–115 cm) based on a bar-stool height of 28 in. (70 cm). Cantilever bar counters out 10 in. (25 cm) to allow room for knees. In a smaller backyard be careful to scale your outdoor kitchen appropriately and do not overweight the size of the counter.

Built-in breakfast counters with high stools can provide an eating area if you do not need or have space for a formal dining table set as part of your kitchen ensemble.

KITCHEN LAYOUTS

A modest outdoor kitchen consists of a built-in propane or charcoal grill set into a 6-ft. (1.8-m) counter with a couple of storage cabinets. This allows enough space to prep and cook, with the flexibility to add additional counter space later on. This is a good place to start if you are unsure of your needs or your budget is restrictive.

Kitchen working surfaces can double as dining tables and should be durable and easy to clean. Materials such as granite, stone tile, decorative concrete and even flagstone are ideal, and the most popular choice for outdoor counters is glazed ceramic tile.

There are three standard choices for a kitchen layout:

- Basic stand-alone counter
- L-shaped return
- U-shape

Tip: Integrate planters into your counters and fill with fast-growing herbs or cut-and-come-again lettuces, a staple of every chef's culinary repertoire. Purple-leaved lettuces with 'Neon Lights' Swiss chard is another beautiful edible duo. Trailing plants such as 'Tumbling Tom' tomatoes look gorgeous cascading over the side of the counter.

KITCHEN MATERIALS

When choosing counter material for your space think about the kinds of weather it will be exposed to—such as snow, rain and constant sunlight. Ask yourself if it will be in close proximity to a grill and exposed to grease stains. High-quality stainless steel provides a sanitary surface, easily cleaned and corrosion resistant in harsh environments but it can get quite hot when exposed to the sun. Natural stone counters such as granite will work well but require regular sealing.

Quartz, the most expensive material, will be relatively maintenance free and durable over the long term; depending on colour it can be a heat sink or reflector.

WALLS, FLOORS AND CEILINGS

Outdoor rooms should have a feeling of enclosure to provide a sense of comfort. This translates into walls, floors and ceilings.

WALLS

Lattice structures are an easy way to create walls while providing support for a variety of striking edibles such as purple beans or cut-and-come-again red-stemmed malabar spinach. Mix with colourful climbing nasturtiums for a festive party space. Climbing peas are a great multi-tasker, supplying peas, of course, but also edible flowers and highly coveted shoots. Planted closely together they can provide a lush green screen on latticework.

Permanent enclosures can be created using prefabricated living walls (see page 47). These vertical structures are packed with soil and can be automatically irrigated, perfect for growing colourful lettuces and herbs. Overhead structure can provide protection as well as opportunity for growing large edible vines such as grapes or kiwis.

Walls can also be expressed using other materials and methods. For an unusual twist that will get your guests talking, plant columnar apples close together so that their foliage overlaps and intertwines like a tunneled arbour. Likewise, espaliered fruit trees trained along a wire fence are a novel as well as artistic way of creating enclosure.

FLOORS

Choose materials and finishes that are not slippery when wet. They should also be stain resistant, easy to clean and durable in harsh weather conditions. Concrete

Use leaf lettuces and herbs to create colourful mosaics of living edible art.

is a natural choice for the outdoor kitchen if it matches your style. Natural stone and concrete unit pavers are also good choices. Whatever you pick, make sure it drains well and is level enough to give you wobble-free outdoor furniture. To protect it from oil and wine spills, maintain your floor with good-quality sealers.

Tip: Choose outdoor kitchen flooring to accent other materials already used on-site or indoors. Use of a similar flooring material that is complementary but different than everywhere else on the property will help to better define the "outdoor room" feel of the barbecue area.

CEILINGS

Retractable awnings and patio umbrellas are the simplest and least expensive overhead shelter for dining and cooking areas. However, for the edible gardener, natural shade from fruit-producing trees and vines is best. Not only do they provide fruit at your fingertips, they also offer shade and are permeable, allowing welcome ventilation and cooling your space.

Pergolas or arbour structures provide support for a variety of climbing colourful edibles. In rainy or colder climates, a pergola topped with Plexiglas panels provides added protection from the elements. Use permanent plantings of vines such as kiwis and grapes.

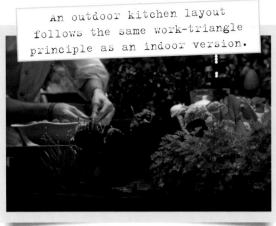

An outdoor kitchen layout follows the same work-triangle principle as an indoor version.

@Aralia Design

Lighting on paths and steps is essential when entertaining outdoors.

©iStockphoto.com/coonoraat

One word of caution: use white-grape varieties, as fruit from red grapes may permanently stain your flooring and equipment.

A simple large fruiting tree can also act as an "organic umbrella." Opt for broader branching cultivars to create an overhead ceiling. Hang outdoor chandeliers, lanterns or miniature strings of lights in the branches for overhead lighting.

ADJACENT SPACES

As outdoor cooking is often a communal experience, you should allocate more space within that zone. In my household, the party always ends up in the kitchen, therefore adjacent casual seating is a must. Dining, lounging, cooking and pool areas often coexist. Think of these as outdoor rooms and consider the flow of traffic between them as you develop a design.

COMFORT AND SEATING

While you don't want to make the outdoors feel just like the inside, you do want to be comfortable and for cold evenings look toward propane patio heaters. Energy-efficient overhead heaters such as infrared quartz units add instantaneous heat with modest electrical output. If your space is fairly small and sheltered from the wind, running the grill can do a

lot to make things comfortable. A firepit also offers warmth and creates a cozy illuminated area to extend your entertaining space. Natural gas patio heaters can be used effectively under eaves and pergolas while portable propane heaters are a good solution for more modest budgets. Radiant heat under the patio and countertops has been used in outdoor kitchens where money is no object.

LIGHTING

Most likely your entertaining will carry over into the evening hours. Providing adequate task lighting in an outdoor kitchen can be quite a challenge. Integrate lighting into overhead structures or into countertops to keep the kitchen working after dark. Provide ambient lighting for the dining area as well. Lighting on paths and steps for safety is also a must.

Tip: For an easy gourmet touch, pluck and serve tender baby vegetables. As nutritious as full-grown vegetables, they offer a more succulent and delicate taste. Most popular with chefs are baby carrots, beets, tiny leaf lettuces and teeny zucchinis with flowers still attached.

Living walls and built-in planters stuffed with trellised edibles create a dramatic and highly functional outdoor room.

A wide variety of closely spaced companion
plants and crops that improve the soil reduces
or eliminates the need for chemical pesticides
and fertilizers.

THE SQUARE FOOT GARDEN

Want to maximize your food with as little space as possible? Want to feed your family something fresh and delicious every day with just a minimal amount of time, energy and room in your garden? I am sure there are not many who would say no to this!

I use the square foot gardening method on my green roof (see page 41) as it is a perfect complement to the formal rectangular beds that house all my (and my neighbours'!) fresh produce. This method of gardening works just about everywhere—from deserts to arid mountain plateaus to cramped urban locations and areas with polluted or high-salinity soils. I grow my edibles in soil less than 10 in. (25 cm) deep!

Simply put, square foot gardening is the practice of creating small but intensively planted raised-bed gardens with a strong emphasis on organic techniques. The term and concept was popularized by Mel Bartholomew in his 1981 book *Square Foot Gardening*.

This method is well suited to beginner gardeners and children, as well as "neat freaks" and those dealing with poor soil, and it is perfect for enabling gardens (see page 93), as the beds are raised.

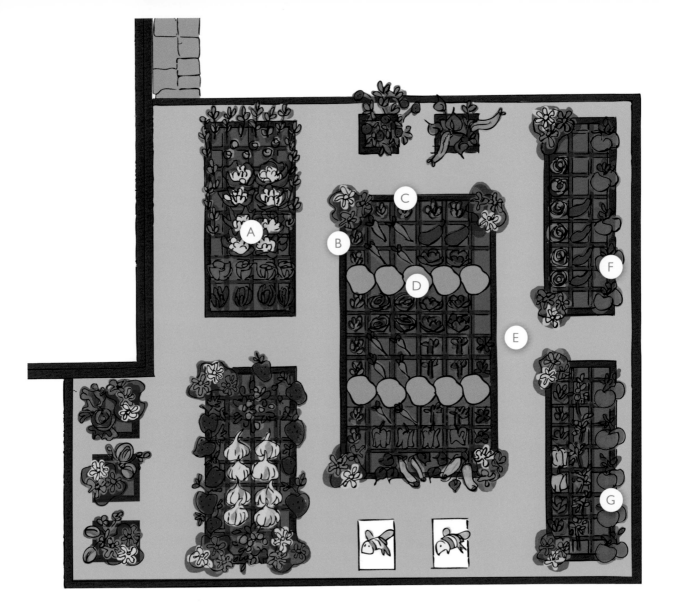

THE PLAN

Area Dimensions: 28 × 24 ft. (7.3 × 8.5 m)

Total Area of Edibles: 250 sq. ft. (23.5 sq. m) in raised beds plus 120 sq. ft. (11.2 sq. m) vertically

The square foot garden principle was used for my edible green roof (see page 41). Five raised planters with only 10 in. (25 cm) of lightweight soil adapted for growing edibles were used.

ADVANTAGES TO CONSIDER

LOOKS GREAT

While some might say that square foot gardening is more technique than style, for those like me who like order and rhythm and geometry in their edible garden, this approach is ideal. And, as an added bonus, it's highly adaptive to formal as well as contemporary garden design.

MORE FOOD IN LESS SPACE

Done correctly, a simple 4 × 4-ft. (1.2 × 1.2-m) block of smaller salad crops will keep one person fed with fresh organic greens throughout the growing season. Two 4 × 4-ft. (1.2 × 1.2-m) blocks will provide that same person with both fresh salad greens and tomatoes, peppers or whatever their choice of longer-season growers.

EASY ACCESS

Narrow beds of 3–4 ft. (90–120 cm) make it easy to work in the garden. For those who wish to plant and weed without bending or squatting, a plywood bottom can be added and the bed positioned on a tabletop or raised platform. This is fantastic for gardeners who are in wheelchairs or required to use a cane or other mobility aid. You can attach wheels to smaller planters

Done correctly, a simple 4 × 4-ft. (1.2 × 1.2-m) block of smaller salad crops will keep one person fed with fresh organic greens throughout the growing season.

to take advantage of sun patterns. And consider adding a cover or cage to protect plants from pests, bright sun or cold weather—in fact, the entire bed can easily be turned into a cold frame to extend your growing season through the fall and winter.

LESS WORK

As raised beds are used, you can easily reach the entire vegetable garden without compacting soil. And because you begin with rich, friable soil, it remains loose and loamy and does not require loosening with heavy tools. Likewise with weeding—the work is reduced because the concept supports densely planted crops that literally shade out weeds before they have a chance to germinate.

©Serga Lindsay

On my green roof, edibles that need deeper soil, such as potatoes or carrots, are grown in a square foot section that has 1-ft. (30-cm) sides.

LESS WATERING

Choose soil augmented with water-holding polymers for planter beds. Retaining large volumes of moisture that is released to plants as required, this soil strategy translates into a less-is-more approach. Hand-watering directly onto plant roots also saves water and keeps foliage dry, reducing the spread of disease.

ALL ORGANIC

Planter beds begin with rich soils and are amended as needed with organic matter and natural fertilizers. The close spacing and wide variety of crops grown, including pest-repelling companion plants (see page 61) and crops that improve the soil (such as nitrogen fixers like peas), makes the system very efficient in terms of reducing or preventing the spread of insects or plant disease. Chemical pesticides and fertilizers are not needed.

DESIGN ELEMENTS

BUILD RAISED BEDS

Raised beds can be made from a wide variety of edging materials (see page 138). The standard reach of a person is about 3 ft. (90 cm) across, therefore beds 4 × 4 ft. (120 × 120 m) can be used if access is from both sides. In total this yields 16 sq. ft. (1.4 sq. m) of edibles. A pathway a minimum of 2 ft. (60 cm) wide (or more as required) encircles the planter. If access is from one side only, a bed 3 ft. (90 cm) wide will allow an easy reach.

Edibles that need deeper soil, such as potatoes or carrots, are grown in a square foot section that has 1-ft. (30-cm) high planter walls.

DIVIDE YOUR BEDS

Each of the beds is divided into square foot units. These can be marked out with sticks, twine, or sturdy slats to ensure they remain visible as the garden matures.

ADD TRELLISES

To be even more efficient in your food production, think about adding a trellis to the north side of the planter beds. I use a frame of PVC pipe strung with netting, with brackets to anchor the bottom ends of the pipe to the side of my planter. This provides a support for plants with runners that normally take up yards of space, such as squash or cucumbers.

PLANTING

Different crops (seeds or seedlings) are planted in each square and the number of squares planted per crop is based on what your favourites are. To encourage variety over time, each square is planted with a different crop than it previously contained. Plant only one seed per hole and space out evenly according to the mature plant size. Although this sounds time consuming, it is actually a time saver. You don't waste minutes or hours (or seed) thinning a thicket of overcrowded seedlings later on. And to harvest, you simply pick the most mature plant from the square—almost like selecting from the produce department at your local grocer!

For maximum efficiency, each of the beds is divided into square foot units marked out with twine, sticks or sturdy slats.

©Serge Lindsay

The square foot principle was used for my edible green roof. Beds are easily accessed from all sides so that every inch of the garden is highly usable; to be even more efficient, a trellis could be added on the north side.

©Serge Lindsay

The number of squares planted per crop depends on what you most want to grow. With each new planting, a different edible is added in each square to reduce the pest and disease problems that can come with repeatedly cultivating the same edibles in the same space.

Plants per 1-ft. (30-cm) Square:

- 1 Plant with 12 × 12-in. (30 × 30-cm) spacing: Broccoli, cabbage, cauliflower, eggplants, peppers, tomatoes (dwarf and vine), squash (vertically), most herbs
- 4 Plants with 4 × 4-in. (10 × 10-cm) spacing: Cucumbers (vertically), lettuce, strawberries, Swiss chard, parsley
- 9 Plants with 3 × 3-in. (8 × 8-cm) spacing: Peas, spinach
- 16 Plants with 2 × 2-in. (5 × 5-cm) spacing: Carrots, onions, radishes

INTERPLANTING

An important concept of square foot gardening is that you can plant two crops simultaneously in the same area. The trick is to be aware of how much room an edible ultimately needs and when it will mature. For example, peppers need one square space. But when first planted a pepper is just a small seedling that takes about 70 days to become a tall, lush bush. So the idea is to utilize all that space around the plant to grow fast-growing crops such as radishes, scallions and even cut-leaf lettuce in the meantime. Tuck a few seeds in the corners of the pepper square and voila! In about 30 days you will have an extra harvest.

MAINTENANCE

General maintenance is similar to traditional edible gardens but on a lesser scale. The techniques for fertilizing and watering, however, vary slightly.

FERTILIZING

Because a new soil mixture is used to create the garden, only a few handfuls of compost are added with each harvest to maintain soil fertility. The state of the soil underlying the raised bed is irrelevant as long as it can drain.

Large plants like cauliflower are grown one to a square, however fast-growing crops can be sowed alongside slower-maturing plants to double the harvest in one space.

WATERING

Hand watering may be required during times of drought even if you use good loamy soil that has high water-retention properties. Otherwise, drip irrigation is best for narrow planters, as this will allow water to be delivered directly at soil level. Avoid conventional pop-up sprinklers that encourage the spread of disease by wetting foliage; plus the overspray can reach your walkways and outdoor living spaces.

You can't go wrong with lettuce from a design, horticultural or edible point of view. The multitude of sizes, shapes, colours and types makes it indispensable for pots and planter beds. Use it to spice up a vegetable row—or plant up a mosaic of colours.

Use your imagination and create your own containers out of recycled materials.

THE CONTAINER GARDEN

Growing food in a container can not only produce a surprisingly abundant harvest but will also add another dimension to any space. I place tall cylinders of bush tomatoes or containers with obelisks of colourful pole beans in my perennial border to add height and texture. On my dining patio I hang pots of 'Tumbling Tom' tomatoes and tuck everbearing strawberries into my permanently planted containers. Pots are also great for filling in any gaps you have in the garden between plantings.

The best part is that you can move containers around to change a mood or vista and the plants in the pots can be revolved seasonally. If you don't want to devote yourself exclusively to food crops, there is a plethora of colourful edibles that will complement your favourite annual flowers.

©Serge Lindsay

Like most edibles, 'Tumbling Tom' tomatoes do best where they receive a minimum of six hours of direct sunshine a day.

©Serge Lindsay

Strawberries complement an *Agave americana* in my outdoor dining room.

DESIGN ELEMENTS

Container gardening is both a craft and an art and allows our imagination the freedom to combine plants of all colours, shapes and textures, as well as match the plants to the pot and display the container where it enhances the garden. Container gardens are the perfect place to experiment with your edibles. If you don't like what you've created, take it apart and start again.

There are certain design principles that are worth noting in order to create that perfect composition.

Tip: For a funky touch, upside down-tomato planters are all the rage and highly functional.

BALANCE AND CONTRAST

Pots and plantings should be in scale to their site. And plants should be the right size for the pots they are planted in, otherwise both will get lost in their respective spaces. In order to look proportionate, plants should not be more than twice the height of the pot or more than one and a half times the width.

Simple plants should be used to show off ornate pots while flamboyant plants are best displayed in simple pots. Whatever you include in your pot, though, remember that it should have at least one thriller, one filler and one spiller.

THRILLERS, SPILLERS AND FILLERS

These three words, coined by garden designer Steve Silk, capture the essence of good container design. Pair this concept with a good colour combination and you have a winning display.

Tip: The only exception to the "thriller, spiller and filler" rule is when you want to show off the colour of a container—in this case, don't hide it with spillers.

Salad plantings can simply
be snipped a leaf at a time
whenever you need some greens.

Swiss chard with its rigid, upright habit and colourful stems screams "attention" and is a "thriller" plant. 'Bright Lights' is like its name—bold and bright. Pair this with vibrant trailing nasturtiums and use rough clay pots for a more casual look (above left).

Or for a more urban and elegant contemporary look, pair 'Fordhook Giant' Swiss chard with white-flowering woolly thyme in a simple black vase-shaped container to set off the monochromatic whites of the stems and flowers (below left).

THRILLERS

Favourites: Swiss chard, upright rosemary, bay topiary, climbing nasturtiums on an obelisk

Container gardens can look one dimensional without a tall plant or two to provide some height. Thrillers are the tall, upright eye-catchers placed either in the centre or off-centre in the container; plant it first. Alternatively, trellises or obelisks for climbing plants can provide height and visual interest.

FILLERS

Favourites: Colourful heirloom lettuce, dwarf cabbages, vivid herbs like yellow oregano, tricolour and purple sages and golden thyme

Good garden design relies heavily on the choice of filler plants and can make or break a composition. Fillers should occupy the mid-ground space without distracting from the thriller, and need to perform well over a long period of time. Great foliage is often the key to a successful filler plant. Colourful or textured leaves can provide interest all season. Plant lower-growing, bushy choices around the centre to give bulk to the planting.

Tip: Nasturtiums are an excellent trap crop for aphids, which they lure away from other edibles. Or you can enjoy the leaves, flowers and seeds in salads!

The colour wheel

SPILLERS

Favourites: 'Tumbling Tom' tomatoes, trailing nasturtiums, everbearing strawberries

Even the nicest container garden is softened and made more cohesive if there are plants flowing over its edges. A great trailer for a pot is one with a long season of interest from fruit or flower.

Tip: For smaller containers, consider dwarf cultivars of your favourite edibles.

COLOUR

Paying attention to your colour palette is the most powerful tool you can use in your container composition. And in addition to the foliage and flower hues, consider the fruit of the edible when you think colour.

For drama and impact, choose hues that are opposite one another on the colour wheel—grouping purple and yellow, for example, makes a powerful statement. For a more tranquil look, stay with varying shades of one colour, such as lavender, lilac and purple.

Tip: 'Royal Burgundy' bush beans are perfect for adding purple to pots and look great with combinations of yellow flowers or foliage.

RED

Favourites: Varieties of lettuce, peppers, Swiss chard and tomatoes

Red is the ultimate for creating drama and excitement. The colour literally reacts with a chemical in our retina and can escalate the body's metabolism. This is why red is ideal for creating fun spaces that scream activity and vibrancy. But beware of using too much, as it can be overwhelming. For more of a party atmosphere pair it with a primary yellow.

YELLOW

Favourites: Varieties of butter beans, nasturtiums, peppers, squash and Swiss chard

The most visible colour, primary yellow is the first the human eye notices! Both breezy and stimulating, a bright and clear yellow leaves a warm and satisfying impression. Contrastingly, dark yellow can be oppressive.

ORANGE

Favourites: Calendula and varieties of marigolds, nasturtiums, peppers, squash and Swiss chard

A good balance between more-intense red and yellow, orange has the cheerful effect of yellow but is intensified.

PINK

Favourites: Varieties of eggplant

Pink represents femininity and symbolizes softness. The use of this colour should be well planned and sparing.

PURPLE

Favourites: Varieties of cabbage, eggplant and kale

A cool shade that symbolizes royalty and dignity, purple is best described as an "unquiet" colour choice.

BLUE

Favourites: Borage, globe artichoke, rosemary, woolly thyme and varieties of eggplant

The second-most powerful colour, blue can represent peacefulness and tranquil contemplation.

GREEN

Favourites: Varieties of lettuce, parsley, and potato foliage

The most restful for the human eye, this universal colour of nature induces calmness.

BLACK

Favourites: A mix of black and white eggplants

Ever-elegant black is a preferred colour in many designs since it contrasts well with most hues and gives a contemporary feel to any design. Match it with white to strengthen that look.

WHITE

Favourites: 'Fordhook Giant' Swiss chard, white-flowering woolly thyme

In the colour spectrum, white is the union of all the colours. Its neutrality and conservative nature make it ideal for establishing clarity and contrast.

PLANTING

Think about where the container will be placed and select plants that require similar growing conditions (such as full sun or shade, moist or dry soil, sheltered or not) yet have different growth habits and bloom times. For high-traffic areas, consider adding fragrant

Tires can be recycled into funky planters. Line with plastic to avoid transfer of potential chemicals.

foliage plants such as lavender, thyme and rosemary where you can enjoy their scent.

POT BASICS

Containers come in a huge variety of materials, colours, sizes and textures. And objects made for other purposes can be re-invented as plant pots, provided they can contain adequate soil for their crops and drainage holes are added. Try a painted garbage can, a clay pot, a large bushel basket or even an old tire! Select pots and materials that complement your garden theme or architecture. If you are unsure, take inspiration from lifestyle and interior-design magazines.

Style	Pot Shape	Pot Colour	Pot Material
Contemporary: Key are smooth matte surfaces and simple shapes	Cylindrical	Black	Aluminum
	Cube	White	Steel
	Rectangle	Red	Fibreglass
		Metal colours	Architectural concrete
		Matte colours	Synthetics: resins and polymers
Rustic/Tuscan	Round	Terracotta	Clay
		Earth colours/ browns	Terracotta
		Clay	Hewn stone
		Wood	Wood
		Stone	
Classic/Heritage	Round rolled rims	Grey	Lead
	Urns	Bronze	Cast resins
	Pots on pedestals	White	

Ensure all your pots have drain holes. Roots need to breath and excess water must drain immediately from them or rot will set in. If you have a container you love that does not drain and prefer it to remain intact, simply fill it with a plant potted up in another container and use it as the drainage tray.

Ensure all containers are stable and heavy enough to resist the wind and not tip over if bumped. For heavy pots you would like to move around or those that need to be brought indoors for winter, wheels or wheeled platforms add portability and spare your back.

If you live in a cooler climate, choose weather-resistant pots. Clay or pottery-type materials may be prone to freezing and cracking in winter weather.

Before you plant, line the bottom of the pot with landscape filter cloth to prevent soil from running out the drain holes. If the pot is large and your edibles do not require much soil depth, use foam peanuts or even pumice (it also holds extra water) to lighten the load.

The rule of thumb for choosing the correct container size is "the bigger the better." Many vegetables don't do well if their roots are restricted, and this is especially true for the squash family. Edibles that don't produce despite being correctly watered and fertilized are usually suffering from restricted roots.

Strawberries and potatoes are attractive and prolific container crops.

Plant	Ideal Pot Diameter
Most herbs	6 in. (15 cm)
Beans, beets, carrots, kale, lettuce, onions, spinach, tomatoes (full)	10 in. (25 cm)
Brussels sprouts, cabbage, chard, collards, kohlrabi, peas, strawberries, turnips	12 in. (30 cm)
Eggplants (dwarf), peppers, squash (summer and winter, dwarf), Swiss chard, tomatoes (dwarf)	10 in. (25 cm) Soil volume of 1–2 gal. (4–8 L) per plant
Blueberries (dwarf), broccoli, cucumbers (full), eggplant (full), pumpkins, squash (summer and winter, full), tomatoes (full)	16 in. (40 cm) Soil volume of 4–5 gal. (16–20 L) per plant

SUPPORTS

Some of your edibles like tomatoes may need support. Tomato cages, although not the most attractive, can do in a pinch and by season's end the plants will most likely cover the wires with their foliage. To dress up cages, consider spray painting the metal with black to visually make it go away or go bold and add in colours that will work with your theme. I have seen a variety of neon blues, yellows, greens and even reds on tomato cages in gardens. For a more traditional look, opt for cone or pyramid-shaped trellises as they usually work better than flat types.

SOIL

Plants in containers are dependent on soil for ample water and nutrients and regular garden soil will not suffice. Use either a soil-less or container mix. Soil-less mixes are readily available and usually labelled as suitable for growing edibles in containers. They are lightweight, well-drained and clean (no diseases or weed seeds). Use a container mix with water-holding gels (starch-based, called "hydrogels") to reduce watering. Change the potting mix every year, as nutrients in the mixture will be used up. And when potting up plants, leave 2–3 in. (5–8 cm) between the top of the soil and the rim of the container to allow water to slowly penetrate the soil to the plants' root systems rather than run off the surface.

LOCATION, LOCATION, LOCATION

Place containers in a spot that gets six hours of direct sun a day. Or, alternatively, select shade-tolerant edibles. And consider positioning your containers so that they can be viewed from indoors or are near seating areas so that you can enjoy your plants—particularly if they are fragrant.

Ensure that your garden provides safe access to containers. Ground-floor materials should be non-slip, non-reflective and fairly level. This means you don't feel a slope under your feet when you stand on that area.

MAINTENANCE

Maintenance can be reduced by good siting of your pots and by choosing plants suitable for container culture and known for pest resistance. Timely upkeep will prevent problems from becoming out of control. Your vegetable containers are best checked daily for insects, mites and signs of disease, with integrated pest management being quickly implemented if needed.

FERTILIZER

There are two types of fertilizers: timed-release and water-soluble. Slow- or timed-release is the easiest to use and is added at planting time—it should be thoroughly incorporated into the soil mix. Look for a complete, balanced type such as a 10-10-10 formulation.

Tip: For those who don't want to worry about adding fertilizer, you can purchase a mix of potting soil that includes timed-release fertilizer.

WATERING

Container plants are more exposed to extremes of weather than are plants in the ground. Even with hydrogels or other organic amendments designed to hold moisture, containers may need daily watering on a very hot day, and some may need it twice a day, particularly as plants mature. Consider using drip irrigation connected to your hose bib with a timer for convenience.

New space-saving cultivars of zucchini make dramatic patio plantings.

Gauge the moisture content of the soil mix by sticking your finger into it; if the soil sticks to your finger, water isn't required.

CONTAINER CLEANUP

With the exception of perennial plantings, at the end of the season, discard the contents of each pot—you do not want to run the risk of spreading disease that may have developed in the soil or foliage. Scrub the container and disinfect it with a 10 percent chlorine-bleach solution.

FINISHING TOUCHES

RAISED BEDS

A raised bed has many advantages over in-ground planting beds and cumulatively this adds up to healthier, more productive plants that yield an earlier harvest. Planters not only give a clean and tidy look but add structure to the landscape. Optimal layouts—beds less than 3-4 ft. (90-120 cm) wide—means space is used efficiently with crops easily accessible from both sides. And because you walk on paths only, the garden is less likely to become compacted so good soil structure and drainage is easy to maintain.

The height of the planter can be adjusted to suit your needs and can translate into less bending as you garden. Soil in raised beds warms up faster in the spring and this enhances plant growth.

Choose from a variety of materials. Untreated wood is most popular because it is easy to work with and inexpensive. Never build raised beds with treated lumber as the toxins can contaminate your food crops. Concrete blocks, natural stone or brick can give your garden a decorative flair but will add to the expense of your project.

Key points to remember while building a raised bed:

- A bed 1 ft. (30 cm) deep provides ample room for most vegetable roots.
- Lining the planting bed with hardware cloth or chicken wire at building time will prevent visits from burrowing animals such as gophers and moles.
- For optimal drainage, over-excavate the base at least 6 in. (15 cm) and backfill with crushed gravel.

WALKWAYS

Most edible gardens require some sort of hard surface for maintaining crops. Surfaces can range from soft materials such as lawn, mulches and wood chips to harder, permanent materials like gravel, concrete, brick and natural stone. Choosing the paving material is usually a matter of personal choice and budget. But be sure it's suitable for its intended use and design aesthetic.

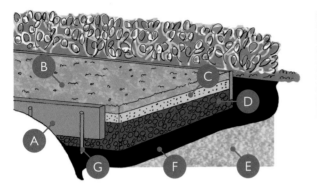

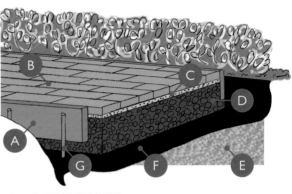

GRAVEL PATHWAY

A Cedar edging (2 × 6)

B Gravel surface compacted

C 2 in. (5 cm) bedding sand

D 2–4 in. (5–10 cm) compacted
gravel (⅜-in. minus crush)

E Compacted sub-base

F Landscape fabric

G 14-in. (35-cm) rebar to hold
edging (1 in./2.5 cm below top)

CONCRETE UNIT PAVERS

A Cedar edging (2 × 6)

B Concrete unit pavers

C 1 in. (2.5 cm) bedding sand

D 6 in. (15 cm) ⅜-in. compacted
gravel (⅜-in. minus crush)

E Compacted sub-base

F Landscape fabric

G 14-in. (35-cm) rebar to hold
edging (1 in./2.5 cm below top)

KEY POINTS WHEN BUILDING GARDEN PATHS

Maintenance access for vegetable gardens needs to be
a minimum of 2–3 ft. (90–120 cm) wide.

Walkways should drain well to prevent puddling.
All hard surfaces should drain away from buildings
and have a slightly raised centre so that the water runs
off the sides.

The foundation for hard surfaces is very important
to prevent heaving (especially in areas that experience
freezing temperatures), which can create tripping
hazards on the surface. A base should typically be 6 in.
(15 cm) deep of compacted gravel.

GRAVEL WALKWAYS

Gravel is a durable mid-range alternative for a
walkway surface. Materials can range from pea
gravel to decomposed granite and rock fines that will
eventually compact down over time to provide an
effect similar to that of concrete.

CONCRETE UNIT PAVERS

Both durable and beautiful, concrete unit pavers are a
higher-range material and off-the-shelf solution that
is easily installed by the homeowner. Pavers come in
a wide range of colours, sizes and designs, and are
adaptable to a variety of landscape styles.

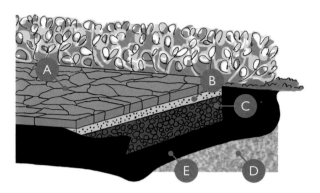

STONE PATHWAY

A   Flagstone (2 in./5 cm thick)

B   2 in. (5 cm) bedding sand

C   4 in. (10 cm) compacted gravel
    (⅜-in. minus crush)

D   Compacted sub-base

E   Landscape fabric

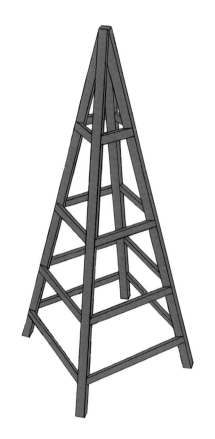

NATURAL STONE

The ultimate walkway, natural stone is often used in high-end garden design. Conveying a sense of elegance and appropriate where curb appeal (think main entrance) is a priority, this material is costly to buy and install.

TRELLISING

Trellises save space and allow you to grow more plants in a given area. Because plants are off the ground, the foliage enjoys better air circulation, minimizing disease. Plants on trellises are exposed to more sunlight so crops ripen faster and fruit is kept out of the reach of hungry slugs.

OBELISK GARDEN TOWER

A garden tower with the crisp geometry of an obelisk adds a stunning focal point and vertical dimension to your garden. Once vines climb onto the obelisk, the contrast between natural and constructed elements will enhance the appeal.

Building the obelisk isn't that difficult if you have good tools and basic carpentry skills. While there are some tricky angled cuts that you'll need to make to get the legs to splay correctly, even if your cuts are off a titch, the tower legs are so long you can flex them slightly to get everything to line up.

A-FRAME TRELLIS

- A   1.5 in. (4 cm) galvanized screws
- B   2 × 3 pressure treated wood, 72 in. (183 cm) long
- C   2 in. (5 cm) galvanized steel pins
- D   2 × 4 pressure treated wood top brace
- E   Screw right angle blocks to top of trellis
- F   Aircraft wire or string tied to top and bottom bars
- G   2 × 3 pressure treated wood, 120 in. (305 cm) long
- H   2 × 4 pressure treated wood brace, placed 59 in. (150 cm) from top

A-FRAME TRELLIS

I designed this A-frame trellis to be a free-standing stable structure that could be taken apart and stored over the winter. I grow five tomato plants on each 10-ft. (3-m) trellis. With luck and good weather, the plants will reach the top bar by August.

Be sure to cut and place the right-angle blocks—they provide structural stability that keeps the trellis from rocking.

Drill pilot holes in the braces of the A-frame; if you want to use wood preservative do so before assembly. If you don't want to treat the wood, use redwood, cedar, white oak, or locust—all woods that will take the elements for some time.

Steel pins are durable and strong, but if you don't want to cut steel rod, use ¼-in. (6-mm) wooden dowels. Bevel the edges so the dowel will fit in with a few taps of a hammer.

It's easiest to assemble the A-frames on a flat surface. When you're ready to put the whole trellis together, have someone hold up the A-frames while you line up the holes with the pins in the ends of the trellis bars.

RESOURCES

To find great information, blogs, videos, inspiration and more, visit the author's websites, *www.sengadesigns.com* and YouTube channel *www.youtube.com/sengalindsay.*

THE TRADITIONAL ROW VEGETABLE GARDEN

WEST DEAN, WEST SUSSEX, UNITED KINGDOM: Beautifully restored Edwardian Kitchen Garden. The gardens are laid out using the classic Victorian design of two cross paths bounded by a perimeter path producing four central beds and a series of borders at the base of the surrounding walls. *www.westdean.org.uk*

A GARDEN FOR CHILDREN

US Source for Edible Children's Gardens. *www.kidsgardening.org*

THE EDIBLE ROOFTOP

Extensive data base on all things related to green roofs and living walls. *www.greenroofs.com*

THE EDIBLE WALL

ATLANTA BOTANICAL GARDENS, ATLANTA, GEORGIA, US: Vertical walls of herbs line the outside circle of an inner garden where vegetables are rotated and grown year round. *www.atlantabotanicalgarden.org*

THE POTAGER GARDEN

CHÂTEAU VILLANDRY, FRANCE: Undoubtedly the world's most famous kitchen garden, this extraordinary design of geometry and symbolism will take your breath away. There are nine different potager garden layouts at Villandry, all the same size, surrounded by a small fence and each symmetrically divided into four quarters, with every bed bordered by short hedges. *www.chateauvillandry.fr*

VERSAILLES, FRANCE: THE POTAGER DU ROI (THE KING'S KITCHEN GARDEN): Located across the street from the Chateau is one of the historically most interesting kitchen gardens and home to a horticultural school and research centre. Pear trees over 200 years old still grow here in a vast variety of topiary forms. The vegetable garden is organically maintained. *www.potager-du-roi.fr*

LE CHATEAU DE ST JEAN DE BEAUREGARD, FRANCE: This is one of France's prettiest kitchen gardens and faithfully restored by its current owners, Monsieur and Madame de Curiel. It is like stepping back into a working kitchen garden of the 16th century—right down to the ancient greenhouses. *www.domsaintjeanbeauregard.com/v2*

THE COMMUNITY GARDEN

FENWAY GARDENS, BOSTON, MASSACHUSETTS, US: The Fenway Victory Gardens are a historic monument and represent the nation's last remaining of the original victory gardens created nationwide during World War II. The gardens encompass an area of 7 acres (3 ha) with more than 500 pots at 15 × 25 ft. (4.5 × 7.5 m) allocated for its citizens to grow vegetable and herbs.
www.fenwayvictorygardens.com

THE HERB GARDEN

SISSINGHURST GARDENS, UK: One of the world's most celebrated gardens and the creation of Vita Sackville-West and her husband Sir Harold Nicholson, this magnificent herb garden was originally laid out in 1933 with the hedges planted a year later.
www.nationaltrust.org.uk/

THE BONNEFONT CLOISTER HERB GARDEN, NY, US: The Bonnefont Cloister in New York City contains more than 250 plant species and typifies what was grown during the Middle Ages. It follows ancient herb garden plans, using raised beds, a central wellhead and what is known as "wattle" fences.
www.metmuseum.org/cloisters

THE ENABLING GARDEN

Chicago Botanic Garden Enabling Garden
www.chicagobotanic.org/explore/enabling.php

THE SQUARE FOOT GARDEN

MEL BARTHOLOMEW, SQUARE FOOT GARDEN: The original developer of this technique and author of the book, *Square Foot Gardening* of the same name, lots of great information and tips.
http://www.squarefootgardening.org

EDIBLE LANDSCAPING